container gardening

DK PAUL WILLIAMS

container
gardening

London, New York, Munich, Melbourne, Delhi

Project editor   Bella Pringle
Project art director   Robin Rout

Set design   John Crummay
Set building   John Crummay & Robin Rout Ltd
                              Gone Wild Ltd

Senior managing editor   Anna Kruger
Senior managing art editor Lee Griffiths
Senior art editor   Alison Donovan
DTP design   Louise Waller
Production controller   Heather Hughes

First published in Great Britain in 2004
by Dorling Kindersley Limited,
80 Strand, London WC2R 0RL

A Penguin company
2 4 6 8 10 9 7 5 3 1

Copyright © 2004
Dorling Kindersley Limited, London

A CIP catalogue record for this book is
available from The British Library

ISBN 1 4053 0269 0

Colour reproduction by Media
Development Printing Ltd, UK

Printed and bound by Tlaciarne BB s.r.o.,
Slovakia

See our complete catalogue at
www.dk.com

Contents

container
introduction

Introduction

Container gardening is both a craft and an art.

It is satisfying to gardeners who, because the plants are seen close up, have the incentive to nurture and cultivate them to a high standard. And because of the portable and contained nature of the plantings, it allows us to grow plants in our gardens that might otherwise be impossible to cultivate because of unsuitable soil or climatic conditions. Container gardening also satisfies the artist within us because it allows our imaginations the freedom to combine plants of all colours, shapes and textures, and to match the plants to the pot, and then place the container display where it benefits the garden most.

It is this combination of the practical and the aesthetic that makes container gardening the most exciting and versatile form of gardening. No matter what your budget, the scale of your garden, or your level of skill or aspiration, you can create a planting that is an expression of your personal taste, a planting that reflects your love of colour or texture, a planting that gives cheer in the gloomiest parts of the garden, and you can grow plants in areas where no soil exists, for example on a balcony or roof terrace.

Bearing in mind that it can honestly be said that any plant can be grown in a pot, the almost unlimited range of plants in the container gardener's palette could be considered daunting. Or you could see it as an opportunity to explore and experiment with any number of combinations of colour and texture; a chance to mix the soft with the hard, the bright with the subdued. This diversity of plant material means that every taste and style can be catered for from the tightest, formal look to the wildest, informal display. Whether you wish to make a statement or simply want some pots that look pretty on the patio, there are pots and plants available to do it with, and to do it with style.

Top left *There has never been such a choice of pots available. Choosing a "special" pot is all part of the pleasure and skill of gardening with containers.*

Top right *How does this look? Matching plant to pot, checking scale and proportion, blending colours and textures: these are just a few of the artistic decisions to make when putting together a container display.*

Bottom left *Abundant plantings such as this thrive when given plenty of care and attention. Take pride in dead-heading flowers regularly and pruning straggly stems, and you will be rewarded with beautiful results.*

Bottom right *Even routine chores, like watering can be enjoyable. I use this opportunity in the evening to mentally relax after a hard day and to check the health of the plants.*

On the following pages, I have brought together a range of plants that I have found useful for creating a wide range of effects. I have grown them all. Some are traditional plants like Lobelias and Impatiens, others are more unusual, such as Plectranthus, which have been chosen in the hope that they will encourage you to search out and experiment with new species. Some plants are hardy and some tender, and most will be found in your local garden centre. Others will need a bit of searching out, but all provide a distinct colour or texture useful in putting together a planting.

I like to compare the skill and the art involved in creating a container planting to that of flower arranging. Most of us have at sometime placed a few flowers in a vase and enjoyed the results. Some of us have taken a little bit more time and arranged the flowers so that they show themselves off to best advantage. A smaller number of us really go to town on flower arranging and are always on the lookout for new flowers or foliage and unusual vases and vessels. There is a lesson to be learned from the "go-ahead" flower arrangers, and I think gardeners could do worse than borrow some of their energy and ideas. But the flower arrangers have an easy time compared to the container gardener. They have the advantage of be able to place their arrangements out of the way of strong winds, baking sun and drenching rain. Florists can always work happily in the knowledge that what they arrange will stay pretty much the same for the life of the display.

The container gardener – with a few exceptions – has to have a vision of how the display will look several months on, when the planting matures. The few small plants planted at the beginning of the season are going to grow and by the end of the summer there will be a container burgeoning with flowers and leaves. In the meantime, you have had to water, feed, prune and pinch out as well as do battle with the pests and diseases that do their best to thwart your efforts. It is not off-putting; it is gardening.

Top left Gardening is all about plants and to be able to grow so many, so well, in such a confined space, is thrilling to the gardener.

Top right Container gardening gives you the opportunity to study close up, details of flowers and foliage that might otherwise go unnoticed.

Bottom left In the confines of a container, the contribution each leaf shape or flower makes becomes an important element in the overall design.

Bottom right Both hardy and tender plants make up the very broad palette of plant species that grow successfully in containers.

container
design

Colour

Container gardening gives you the opportunity to be very specific in your choice and use of colour.

Plants in pots are in intimate contact with each other and their area of display is confined. So, in container plantings, the subtle colour details and combinations that might easily become lost in a border setting are there to be appreciated, right in front of you.

If you are unsure about how to use colour in your plantings, take inspiration from lifestyle and interiors magazines and translate what you find there into ideas for plant and container colours. And try the following colour combinations that I find work well. White is extremely versatile: with green it achieves a unique freshness; with yellow and green it is cool and lively; with pinks and blues it has a romantic feel; and it really sets off bright colours such as oranges and reds.

Purple works in many combinations: with grey and pink it is sophisticated; with yellow more light-hearted; with brown it is sombre but classy; with crimson it can appear regal; with orange, jazzy; and with white, cool. Blue as a flower colour is in short supply, but any element of blue in a planting is eye-catching. Reds, yellows, and oranges are ideal for flamboyant displays; with magenta and violet they make vivacious mixes.

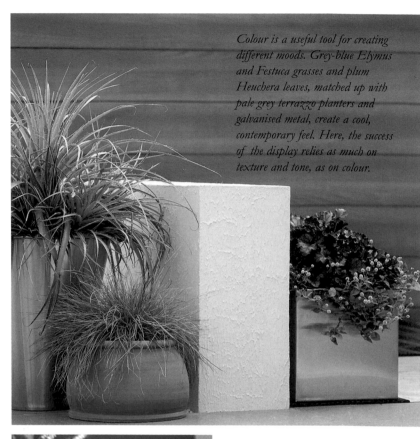

Colour is a useful tool for creating different moods. Grey-blue Elymus and Festuca grasses and plum Heuchera leaves, matched up with pale grey terrazzo planters and galvanised metal, create a cool, contemporary feel. Here, the success of the display relies as much on texture and tone, as on colour.

Combinations using just one plant and pot colour in all the containers are an easy and direct way to produce a purposeful display. Here, traditional terracotta and a moulded resin "studded" pot have been used in combination with fiery orange Isoplexis and Cuphea to create a Mediterranean-style terrace.

Limiting the planting scheme to just one or two colours is by far the easiest way to give your containers a designed look. By planning out the colour palette in this way, the whole display becomes more focused and unified. Here, purple Salvias, magenta Tibouchina and magenta and white Impatiens have been chosen to create the desired colour effect.

There are times when you want out-and-out exuberance and this is best achieved using a riotous mix of colours where no rules apply. Make maximum use of the container colour and look for plant material in bright and contrasting hues. Here, a vibrant display is achieved by grouping one-colour and one-species plantings together to give you the flexibility to switch between the two styles.

Texture

The sole aim of ornamental gardening is to excite the senses and bring us pleasure.

Plants with textural foliage not only stimulate us visually, but also invite us to get up close and touch them. Inevitably, you will want to feel or caress their leaves to see if they are as smooth, silky, rough, hard, soft or spiky as they look. The opportunity to experience pleasurable tactile sensations is definitely one of the joys of gardening.

As a container gardener, you can work with the range and interplay of textures by putting together plants with a similar feel such as those with soft and furry leaves and stems, or those that are fleshy and smooth. You can also develop interesting contrasts of texture by planting the hard and smooth next to the soft and velvet-like. Through the textures of the plantings that you use within a given space, different moods and effects can be created. Sharp, spiky plants make for a lively and energetic atmosphere, while softer more pliable plants induce a more relaxed and mellow feel. These principles apply not only to foliage but also to flowering plants. And always remember to include the container in the equation. Select a material or a finish that will enhance your textural planting and produce a distinctive display.

The artistic gardener has to be resourceful and remember that not only the colour but the texture of the plant material can produce fabulous results. This simple two-plant combination could be quite ordinary but for the energy supplied by the grasses wispy, untamed appearance. Their tangled mass makes you want to comb your hands through the strands and caress the soft seedheads.

There are a few instances where one plant offers a perfect blend of all the features of texture, colour, and balance we are trying to create with a mix of plants. The Japanese painted fern (Athyrium niponicum var pictum) shown here, combines all the attributes I could wish for – a sophisticated, harmonious pink, grey and green colour scheme, a balanced shape and a soft, interesting texture.

In the plant world, texture, colour and shape are closely linked as many of the plant characteristics have developed together in response to environmental factors. Here, the strap-like leaves of Phormium have a shiny surface and are set against the matt finish of the cast-iron container. Though these details of texture are small, without them the effect of this planting would be diminished.

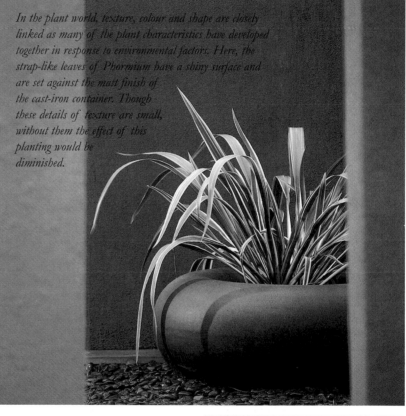

Plantings that rely solely on texture have a sophistication that is hard to beat. I enjoy them because the display is carried by the distinctive character of the leaves. Here, I have used two extremes of leaf size and texture. The large Kalanchoe leaves are furry and could not be more different than the feathery foliage of Lotus maculatus and L. berthelotti and the speckled fleshy pennies of trailing Cerapegia.

Scale and proportion

Getting these two important design elements right is one of the greatest challenges of container gardening.

The proportions of every planting are constantly changing as plants grow and mature. This certainly presents a problem for container gardeners who must try to see the finished display in their mind's eye when planting: a difficult task when young plants, at this stage, may be less than a quarter of their eventual size.

When planning the scale and proportion of a display, it is important to consider the growth habit of the species you have chosen; this will help you work out how the planting will look over time.

For standard designs, which feature a tall central plant in a round pot, ideally the finished height should be between one and one-and-a-half times the height of the container, and the planting roughly triangular in shape. But this proportion of container to planting is not a rigid rule to be applied in every instance. When you look through the chapter on Container Portraits *(see pages 26-115)* you will see that it is a flexible guideline to be adapted according to the shape of the container. Generally, I try to avoid large plantings in pots with narrow bases as they upset the eye by appearing top-heavy, while the same plants in a wide-based pot look stable and pleasing.

Traditional container planting designs use a tall plant in the centre to balance the pot height and to create a focus for the display. With smaller, rounded pots, it is best to avoid height in the centre as it makes low arrangements look top heavy. Instead, create a dome-shaped design that can be enjoyed from all angles. Here, Tradescantia and Ageratum work to make a well-balanced, planting.

This low-level planting of Echeveria takes a significant but secondary role, allowing the pot's large size and rounded shape to dominate the design. It's smooth, curved shape is accentuated by this low surface planting of succulent leaves. This choice of planting helps to keep the whole display's centre of gravity low and creates an overall effect of stability, security and solidity.

These two very different pot sizes and shapes sit against their own wall but work well together. The choice of plants and clever play on scale, helps accentuate the shape of the pots, but I would prefer the grass to be shorter and the Agave bigger for balance.

Balance tall narrow pots with tall plants that are at least twice the height of the pot. Ideal subjects include the grasses Molinia caerulea *subsp* arundinacea 'Bergfreund' and varieties of Miscanthus sinensis *as they offer height, grace, and a lightness that does not challenge the weight of the pot. Alternatively, choose a broad and full plant that does not grow above half the height of the pot to balance the proportions. Here, I have used the hardy* Fuchsia magellanica *'Versicolor'. Trailing plants help visually reduce the scale of tall pots but use them with a tall companion plant for best effect.*

Shape

Careful use of shape can help to create drama and excitment, or calmness and serenity.

The most obvious expression of shape in the container garden is topiary, where plants are clipped into geometric or fanciful shapes for effect. Less manicured expressions of shape, however, can be achieved by using plants with large or distinctive leaves or imposing arrangements of branches and stems. These "architectural" plants often work best when used on their own in containers, rather than as a mixed group, so that their shape really stands out. Indeed, a single well-shaped plant can have sufficient presence to stand alone as the centrepiece of a small courtyard or patio garden.

When grown in containers, plants such as *Mahonia japonica*, *Aralia elata* 'Variegata' Aucuba, Yucca, Cordyline, Phormium, *Acer palmatum* 'Dissectum', *Rhus glabra*, *Fatsia japonica* and many palms and bamboos offer a wide range of foliage and shapes to enhance a garden design. Effective on their own as garden focal points, they also work well as the main feature in a larger group of pots.

When relying on plant shapes to create impact, avoid unduly fussy pots as the detail will detract from the main theme. Pots with simple outlines and strong shapes will work much better.

Plants that rely on shape and structure rather than flowers for their effect are of great value to the container gardener when creating simple, modern displays. They are most effective when used in uncluttered surroundings with few other visual distractions.

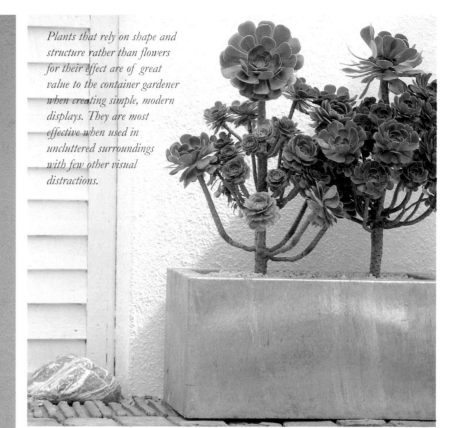

For dramatic impact, use bold simple shapes and keep plant and pot colours to a minimum. I find that by combining just two or three simple shapes, I can create maximum impact. Here, the bulbous pot shape and the branching cactus echo one another. To achieve the same effect as this tender cactus in a colder climate, choose a hardy Ilex crenata that has been clipped into a "cloud tree" shape.

In my experience, curved lines and rounded shapes in the garden create a more relaxed, informal atmosphere and promote feelings of calm. I like to use curved handmade pot shapes, as shown here, in conjunction with willowy plants like bamboo or the smaller, arching leaves of grasses, such as Stipa arundinacea, S. tennuissima and Hakonechloa macra to engender this atmosphere of tranquility.

Shape can be used to create different moods within a garden space. Here, the shape of this finely balanced stainless-steel container creates a mood of fragility and instability as it sits on its pointed end. The spreading nature of the plants further exaggerates the balancing act. Squat and dumpy shapes create the exact opposite effect – that of solidity and assuredness.

Repetition

In the container garden, repeating patterns and symmetry are pleasing to the eye and comfort the mind.

Repetition and symmetry are design elements that are fundamental to most of the great gardens with their avenues of trees, balustrades, steps, topiary, and knot gardens. Seeing a single component repeated over and over again does instil a feeling of abundance and prosperity. Rows of large potted orange trees, for example, flanking a walkway are an impressive sight. While most of us cannot emulate the scale of grand designs, we can certainly apply the idea to our own, more modest gardens, to create a sense of largesse and comfort. Even on a small-scale, identical repeated plantings engender admiration and convey a suggestion of wealth. Rows of pots can also be used to emphasise or exaggerate perspective along a path or a walkway, and you can transform an ordinary rise of three or four garden steps into a grand entrance by placing an identical pot at either end of each step. Repeated plantings can be incorporated among the plants in a border. Use large containers that stand above the existing planting and place them along the length to create continuity and give the border coherence. Harmonising the container planting with the border either by colour or style will also enhance the overall effect.

By using the same pots and plants in a row, the design takes on a formal, almost regimental precision. The pots are tall enough to act as a barrier and can be used to mark off areas of the garden and help define the space. I like to think of them as traffic cones! When placed alongside a path, a row of identical pots can even make an ordinary walkway appear quite special.

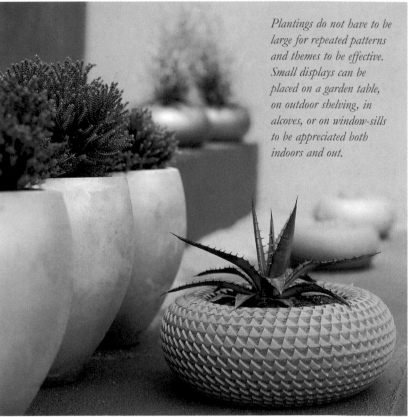

Plantings do not have to be large for repeated patterns and themes to be effective. Small displays can be placed on a garden table, on outdoor shelving, in alcoves, or on window-sills to be appreciated both indoors and out.

Here, repetition is treated in a slightly different way. The same pot and plant materials are repeated but the container and plant shapes are different. Box topiary in ball shapes and spirals is planted in terrazzo containers of different shapes and sizes. A mirror effect adds to the repetition of the design as the pots sit in front of a reflective stainless-steel surface.

This row of identical pots filled with hardy, abundant plantings transforms a plain paved yard and will last throughout the year. Each pot is planted up with Heuchera, Stipa arundinacea *and* Carex *'Evergold'.*

Grouping

Moving pots around, trying them this way, trying them that way, is one of the joys of container gardening.

With careful positioning, a group of disparate pots can be built into a cohesive, arrangement that has far greater impact than the sum of the individual pots.

Grouping pots together is a great opportunity to make the most of their varying heights and styles. The other advantage of groups is that any gaps created by less mature plantings can be successfully disguised through skilful placing and overlapping.

In creating container groupings you are combining the principles of balance, shape and proportion that you have already applied to an individual planting. A group arrangement also has more potential, giving you the flexibility to constantly rearrange the individual pots for maximum effect.

As the plants start to grow taller and begin to fill out, move the pots apart slightly to give each planting the chance to develop fully and to create a more sumptuous display.

To add variety of height to your grouping, consider raising some of the pots on other upturned pots or stand them on shelves. This is particularly useful for smaller pots, making them more visible and increasing their stature.

Successful colour and texture effects can be quickly achieved by bringing together groups of pots containing different plant species. This method is ideal for combinations of plants where one of the species might only look its best for a few weeks. When a plant is at its peak, quickly manoeuvre it into place next to a complementary planting for maximum effect.

By grouping plants from a similar habitat or climate, you can recreate the essence of that environment. Here, a large vine is placed alongside an olive tree. Pots of lavender, rosemary and other sun-loving plants could also be introduced to recreate a warm, dry, Mediterranean-style garden.

Placing pots and plantings of similar style and colour together can engender a specific mood within a given part of the garden. Here, a white stone urn, a terracotta pot, and the use of delicate foliage and pink flowers, such as Pelargoniums, creates a country-style feeling of freshness and cool.

Small pots like these can be easily moved and rearranged as plants come into flower and then go over. By growing only one type of plant in each pot, there is huge scope to keep reorganising the group to create the best combination of height, colour and texture. A tableau like this can be constantly refreshed.

container
portraits

Sunset shape

If I had to choose one leaf or flower colour above all others for container gardening it would be purple.

INGREDIENTS	QTY
Agastache 'Apricot Sprite'	× 4
Cordyline australis Purpurea Group	× 1
Lavandula 'Fathead'	× 2

In my view, purple is invaluable to the gardener. It is a very versatile colour with the ability to harmonise with almost all flowers and foliage. Many plant species are available in purple tones and these offer an unimaginable variety of textures and shapes to add interest to container plantings. Here, the smooth shiny aubergine coloured pot is set against matt purple Cordyline leaves, while a band of soft grey Agastache foliage and apricot Agastache flowers act as a go between – delicious. In the background, the bumble-bee heads of the French lavender (*Lavandula* 'Fathead'), make a subtle link between the shiny plum pot and the softer purple Cordyline foliage.

Agastache 'Apricot Sprite' See p.158

PLANTING DETAILS

Planting plan No clever planning here. The Cordyline goes in the centre of the pot, and the four Agastaches are planted around it, leaving space for the two Lavenders on either side at the back. Bear in mind that Cordyline leaves can vary in colour from purple to brown. This one has distinctly purple leaves and I think that it is worth the effort tracking down a good purple colour form.

Plant care Technically speaking, this planting should be classified as tender but if it is kept in a warm, sheltered site the Cordyline and Lavender will live through the winter. Only the Agastache will die back in winter but it will shoot again in spring.

Cordyline australis Purpurea Group See p.165

CONTAINER DETAILS

Style and **Shape** The glazed ceramic pot is a rich aubergine colour and a considerable size which gives it a strong presence in the garden. When viewed from standing height, the planting and, particularly the dense Cordyline in the centre, appears more in balance with the pot size. With a large, cylindrical container, try to achieve a planting at least as high as the pot is deep to maintain good proportions.

Size Height 53cm (21in); Diameter 45cm (18in).

Material Frostproof glazed ceramic.

Lavandula 'Fathead' See p.172

Scarlet and black

Colour has a powerful impact. Here, deep flower and foliage colours create a wonderful moody display.

INGREDIENTS	QTY
Dahlia 'Roxy'	× 3
Pelargonium 'Harvard'	× 4
Persicaria microcephala 'Red Dragon'	× 1
Rhodochiton atrosanguineus	× 1
Sambucus nigra 'Black Lace'	× 1

There are many ways of displaying this sophisticated container planting to best effect outdoors. Its strong, dark colour palette will create a dramatic statement when set against a flower border of deep purple-red Peonies, dark blue Delphiniums or the drooping flower spikes of *Buddleia* 'Black Knight'. This deep-coloured planting can also be used in an area of the garden where flowers and foliage, or even the hard landscaping reflect more light into the planting to bring the darker flower and foliage colours into sharp relief.

Dahlia 'Roxy'   See p.166

Pelargonium 'Harvard'   See p.176

PLANTING DETAILS

Planting plan This is one of my favourite colour plantings but for one item; the yellow centres of the Dahlia flowers upset the carefully planned colour balance. Pedantic? Maybe. The rest of the planting is a moody blend of purples and reds with lightening touches of fresh green provided by the Pelargonium leaves. While the feathery Sambucus foliage at the back balances the heavier Dahlia foliage decorating the front. The Sambucus also provides physical support for the more delicate Rhodochiton stems while the Persicaria pokes its strong shoots through it all.

Plant care If the Persicaria leaves get too rampant, pinch out their growing tips.

Persicaria microcephala 'Red Dragon'   See p.177

CONTAINER DETAILS

Style and **Shape** I like this pot. A broad top and narrow base gives it a funnel-like shape, which you might think is unstable, but its base is wide enough to make it stand firm. The funnel shape allows for plenty of front-to-back depth in the planting as well as providing room for a large volume of potting compost so that the plants grow strong and healthy.

Size Height 50cm (20in); Diameter 60cm (24in).

Material Galvanised steel.

Rhodochiton atrosanguineus   See p.180

Sambucus nigra 'Black Lace'　　　　See p.180

Modern black

Black on white is the ultimate in monochromatic contrast and produces a very startling modern effect.

INGREDIENTS	QTY
Aeonium 'Zwartkop'	× 1
Ipomoea batatas 'Blackie'	× 3
Ophiopogon planiscapus 'Nigrescens'	× 5

Black and white is a classic design combination and I thought it would be an exciting challenge to reproduce this colour scheme with plants. White flowers come with green leaves and stems – which I didn't want – so instead I decided to get my pure, unadulterated white from the pot surface while relying on plants with black leaves and stems to do the rest. But black also posed a problem because I'm not convinced that any plant really is true black. Though many varieties are labelled as "black" most are just very dark shades of purple or red, as is the case with Aeonium and Ipomoea. However, I do think *Ophiopogon planiscapus* 'Nigrescens' is the best "black" there is in the plant world for container gardening.

Aeonium 'Zwartkop' See p.158

PLANTING DETAILS

Planting plan Having decided on using just "black" plants it could almost be said that this display chose itself because of the very limited choice of large plant subjects available in this colour. *Aeonium* 'Zwartkop' was an automatic choice for its height and shape. *O. planiscapus* 'Nigrescens' had to be included because of its depth of blackness. The non-climbing Ipomoea was chosen for its wonderful leaf shape and deep, deep colour. When positioning this planting remember that the whiter the surroundings, the darker the foliage will appear.
Plant care Plenty of sunshine will keep the plant foliage at its blackest.

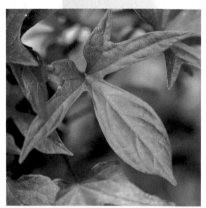
Ipomoea batatas 'Blackie' See p.171

CONTAINER DETAILS

Style and **Shape** I decided to use a pot which was pure white but had a rough texture to give it some warmth. I thought that a marble-smooth white surface would have made the whole display look too cold and clinical. This container planting is small enough in scale to sit on a modern garden table or, for even greater effect, in an alcove in a white stucco wall.
Size Height 30cm (12in); Diameter 40cm (16in).
Material White stone composite.

Ophiopogon planiscapus 'Nigrescens' See p.174

Light and shade

Few flowers are to be had in winter so strong leaf shapes are important for all-year-round plantings.

INGREDIENTS	QTY
Heuchera 'Can-can'	× 3
Juncus effusus f. *spiralis*	× 1
Teucrium scorodonia 'Crispum'	× 3

This dark plum and fresh green planting satisfies the need for texture, shape, and colour in the garden during the winter months by successfully mixing the evergreen foliage of three hardy plants. The pale green crinkled-edged leaves of Teucrium act as a foil for the dark plum-veined leaves of Heuchera, whilst the twisted Juncus stems fire out from the heart of the planting with vitality and humour.

In summer, this planting earns its place in the garden by providing a shade-tolerant mix of flower and foliage. I find that shady corners are often neglected during the summer and look bare during the winter when the rest of the garden is dormant. This effective planting offers a good, all-year-round solution.

Heuchera 'Can-can'   See p.171

PLANTING DETAILS

Planting plan The *Juncus effusus* f. *spiralis* forms the central plant in this design and is planted up in the middle of the pot. The Heucheras and Teucriums are then planted alternately around the edge of the container.

Plant care Plants sited in shady corners are often overhung by trees or shrubs and so are sheltered from the rain and may dry out. Do not forget to water them. *Teucrium scorodonia* 'Crispum' is a rambling plant that will need trimming to prevent it from engulfing its neighbours. In sheltered spots, the Heuchera will produce vertical spires of flowers for several months which look good set against the curly Juncus stems.

Juncus effusus f. *spiralis*   See p.172

CONTAINER DETAILS

Style and **Shape** This low container is intended for a site at the top of a flight of garden steps so that it can be seen as you walk up or down. Alternatively, place it close to a favourite garden ornament or sculpture. The display will add some complementary or heartening greenery throughout the winter months.

Size Height 40cm (16in); Diameter 50cm (20in).

Material Handmade frostproof terracotta.

Teucrium scorodonia 'Crispum'   See p.182

Cool and fresh

Simple colours and clean lines create a refreshing blend. This planting makes good use of both.

INGREDIENTS	QTY
Chlorophytum comosum 'Variegatum'	× 3
Cordyline australis	× 1
Cuphea hyssopifolia 'Alba'	× 3
Impatiens 'Accent White'	× 6
Plectranthus madagascariensis Variegated mintleaf	× 4

Taking inspiration from the pure white pot, the structure of this planting is simple as is the colour – just greens and whites. *Cordyline australis* must surely have been designed for the container gardener; take a pot, place a Cordyline in the middle and you are half way there.

The only other consideration is what to put around it. To avoid a stark effect, the sword-like leaves need a balancing softness. Here I have used a variegated Plectranthus that arches gracefully as it flows out of the pot but is substantial enough to balance the strong shape of the Cordyline. This combination suits sun or shade but is at its best where its lightness can lift a shady area.

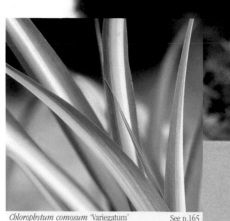

Chlorophytum comosum 'Variegatum' See p.165

Cordyline australis See p.164

PLANTING DETAILS

Planting plan Tucked in amongst the Plectranthus is a mix of frothy white Cuphea and large, glistening white Impatiens. To stop the Cuphea and Impatiens becoming an amorphous jumble there are three plants of the very common variegated Chlorophytum spiking their way through, echoing the shape of the Cordyline leaves.
Plant care Deadhead Impatiens regularly and remove any split or discoloured stems from the Chlorophytum, as they age.

Cuphea hyssopifolia 'Alba' See p.166

CONTAINER DETAILS

Style and **Shape** This smooth terrazzo pot has a marble-like coolness that is given an extra chill by its white colouring. I have used soothing, complementary greens, but you could also try bright contrasting colours. To balance the pot and planting, the Cordyline was chosen to be at least as tall as the pot is deep. The broad base of the pot gives it a stable look but it still retains some elegance and it can hold plenty of compost – very important when relying on foliage for effect.
Size Height 60cm (24in); Diameter 60cm (24in).
Material White terrazzo.

Impatiens 'Accent White' See p.170

Plectranthus madagascariensis Var'd mintleaf   See p.179

Rampaging reds

United by a well-planned colour scheme, hardy shrubs and tender perennials will mix happily.

INGREDIENTS	QTY
Euonymus fortunei 'Emerald 'n' Gold'	× 1
Petunia 'Trailing Red'	× 3
Sambucus nigra 'Black Lace'	× 1
Solenostemon 'Midnight'	× 1
Verbena 'Aztec Red Trailing'	× 3

Hardy plants have different characters and needs to tender plants and sometimes these are so different that it seems strange to find them alongside one another in a mixed planting. It is a clash that is hard to explain and perhaps one only noticed by experienced gardeners who are familiar with the hardiness of their plants and realise when they make uneasy bedfellows. Here, two very different hardy shrubs are successfully combined with tender plants using an overall colour theme to bring all the elements – pot included – together. The lacy Sambucus leaves add a wispy topping to balance the full red skirt of Petunia and Verbena flowers.

Euonymus fortunei 'Emerald 'n' Gold' See p.168

Petunia 'Trailing Red' See p.179

PLANTING DETAILS

Planting plan Neither the Euonymus nor Sambucus is going to get much bigger during one growing season so choose sufficiently large plants to start with. Choose a Sambucus as tall as the pot is deep. Plant these two main elements first with the variegated Euonymus in the middle of the pot in front of the Sambucus. Position the Solenostemon in front of the Euonymus then fill in with Petunias and Verbenas. I like to use variegated foliage like Euonymus in pots because I think their unnatural looking leaf colour and slightly exotic nature are of benefit in container plantings while making them difficult to reconcile in a garden scheme.
Plant care The Petunias and Verbena need regular deadheading.

Sambucus nigra 'Black Lace' See p.180

CONTAINER DETAILS

Style and **Shape** The pot has a high shine finish that almost defies outdoor use. I have used vibrant reds to draw attention away from its high gloss finish whilst using darker Solenostemon leaf colour in the middle and top of the planting to spread and diffuse a depth of colour through the whole arrangement.
Size Height 45cm (18in); Width 45cm (18in).
Material Black glazed ceramic.

Solenostemon 'Midnight' See p.182

Verbena 'Aztec Red Trailing'   See p.185

Sculptural shapes

*Single, stand alone, elements can be brought together
to create a stunning group for far-reaching impact.*

INGREDIENTS *left container*	QTY
Phormium hybrid	× 1
INGREDIENTS *centre container*	QTY
Solenostemon 'Winter Sun'	× 1
INGREDIENTS *right container*	QTY
Canna 'Durban'	× 1

Any one of these planted pots looks balanced and stylish on its own but bring them together and they have an impact that is far greater than they would have individually. The colours and shapes of the plants and containers have been carefully selected to harmonise and bring a balance to the whole. Grouping containers provides an opportunity to play with height, scale and proportion, colour and shape. By giving thought to the juxtaposition of pots and plants a collection of ordinary looking plantings can be turned into an arrangement that is making a statement not just about itself but about you and your skills as an accomplished container gardener.

Canna 'Durban' See p.163

Phormium hybrid See p.178

PLANTING DETAILS

Planting plan These rusty iron containers share a common style but each planting has been carefully thought out to complement its neighbours' leaf shape and character, while a contemporary warm orange colour scheme links the vibrant leafy foliage in all three pots and the rusty iron containers.

Plant care These are all sun-loving plants. The Canna and Solenostemon benefit from being sheltered from the wind. Wind-protection will prevent the large leaves of the Canna from becoming ragged and ensure that the slightly brittle branches of the Solenostemon do not snap off as the plant grows.

CONTAINER DETAILS

Style and **Shape** These tall planters are hollow to reduce their weight, but they are still robust and well-balanced. Each pot has a smaller square metal box welded inside and these have sufficient space for one plant to grow well, which suits their simple style. The interest is created by the way the pots are grouped.

Size Height 110cm (44in); Width 50cm (20in) *(large planter)*.
Height 100cm (40in); Width 40cm (16in) *(medium planter)*.
Height 70cm (28in); Width 50cm (20in) *(small planter)*.
Material Rusty iron.

Solenostemon 'Winter Sun' See p.183

Shimmering silvers

Despite its ability to tolerate the hottest sunshine, this gleaming silver display presents an icy coolness.

INGREDIENTS	QTY
Convolvulus cneorum	× 3
Leymus arenarius	× 3
Silene uniflora 'Swan Lake'	× 2

Plants with grey or silver leaves offer a clear signal to the gardener that a species is tolerant of hot and dry conditions. Here two graceful and charming white-flowered plants, Convolulus and Silene, grow alongside Leymus, a strikingly coloured and fast-growing grass. Though only 50cm (20in) square, the gleaming white terrazzo container looks very substantial and illustrates the solid, "settled" effect that can be achieved using straight-sided planters. This display looks good set in a sleek, minimalist garden setting but also in the midst of lush greenery, where the white and silver flower and foliage colours will stand out from the background.

Convolvulus cneorum See p.164

PLANTING DETAILS

Planting plan This is a front-facing display, so the tall grasses are planted along the back edge of the container, while the Convolvulus occupies the middle, and the Silene is planted at the front of the pot so that it can trail over the edge.

Plant care This is a hardy perennial planting that would last for many years if it wasn't for the fact that Leymus is very invasive, and, given the chance, it will take over the whole pot in one or two seasons. To prevent this, break up the planting at the end of the season, take out most of the Leymus and remake the display. I also cut off the Leymus flowers early before they turn brown.

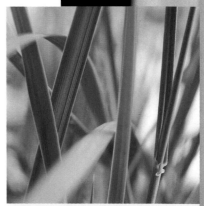
Leymus arenarius See p.173

CONTAINER DETAILS

Style and **Shape** Square pots allow for a large volume of potting compost and offer plenty of space for plant growth. Here, there is room for the Leymus grass to run around before it starts to overwhelm the other plants. While the grass is growing to its full height, the design appears to be bottom heavy. To help redress this inbalance, I have planted a frill of dangling *Silene uniflora* 'Swan Lake' whose white, ballet dancer's tutu-like flowers help interrupt the massive scale of the pot.

Size Height 50cm (20in); Width 50cm (20in).

Material White terrazzo.

Silene uniflora 'Swan Lake' See p.181

Abundant style

A busy plant mix creates a floriferous display with a cascade of white flowers through the season.

INGREDIENTS	QTY
Abutilon 'Nabob'	× 1
Helichrysum petiolare	× 2
Helichrysum petiolare 'Limelight'	× 2
Petunia 'Trailing White'	× 3
Verbena Tapien Violet	× 3

I have chosen a selection of vigorous plants that have quickly filled out this large terracotta urn and tumbled over the edge. If left untamed, they will eventually cover up the pot completely. In this "all-in-style", the plants intermingle creating a jumbled mass of foliage and flower. There is always a danger of a planting like this becoming completely shapeless with no visual points of reference to hold the eye. The tall column of large Abutilon leaves in the centre of the display help counter this by giving the arrangement some structure and, if the silvery Helichrysum foliage is encouraged to work its way through the trailing white Petunias, it will break up this mass of flowers.

PLANTING DETAILS

Planting plan This is an all-round arrangement to be seen from every angle. The Abutilon occupies the centre and the Petunias and Verbenas are spaced equally around the Abutilon working out towards the rim. The Helichrysums are planted, equally spaced between the edge of the pot and the centre.

Plant care Too much of any one element is not desirable in a mixed planting so keep watch. Thin out the trailing Petunia occasionally. It is a very vigorous plant and will overwhelm the Verbena and Helichrysum if not kept under control. Also keep the Helichrysum in check to prevent too much foliage covering the Abutilon.

CONTAINER DETAILS

Style and **Shape** Though only filled to half its depth to keep the large terracotta urn's weight to a minimum, this container holds plenty of potting compost to support these fast-growing plants. As the plants get bigger, they will need more and more water. Add that to the fact that terracotta is porous and speeds up water evaporation and you need to take care not to let the potting compost dry out too quickly.

Size Height 80cm (32in); Diameter 60cm (24in).

Material Terracotta.

Abutilon 'Nabob' See p.157

Helichrysum petiolare See p.170

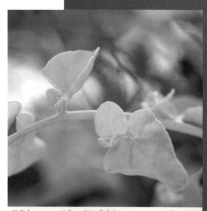

Helichrysum petiolare 'Limelight' See p.170

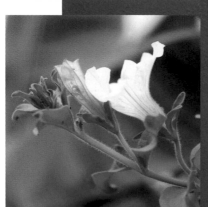

Petunia 'Trailing White' See p.179

Verbena Tapien Violet   See p.184

Trailing purples

Using flowers within a limited colour range ties a scheme together regardless of the choice of plants.

INGREDIENTS	QTY
Salvia splendens 'Purple'	× 5
Verbena 'Diamond Merci'	× 2
Verbena Tapien Violet	× 1
Viola 'Bowles' Black'	× 2

Here, the purple and violet flowering plants have been carefully selected to work well together and to match the grey and blue metallic finish of the planter. To maintain a good sense of proportion, the flowering spires of the Salvias are balanced by the trailing stems of Verbena. The dark metal base of the trough anchors the display and prevents the tall Salvias from making the arrangement appear top heavy. Within such a scheme, I like to add one element, however small, that bends the rules; a small detail that has to be discovered. Here, it is the black Violas which register as tiny holes of black velvet amongst the busy foliage.

PLANTING DETAILS

Planting plan This narrow trough has little space from front to back so the Salvias are packed in as tightly to the back edge as possible. The Verbenas are spaced evenly along the front of the trough leaving small pockets to tuck in the Violas.

Plant care There is a lot of plant material in a relatively small container so regular fortnightly feeding is important to maintain healthy plants. Pinch out the tips of the Verbenas when they are still small to encourage bushy growth and deadhead the flowers regularly to encourage more to grow.

CONTAINER DETAILS

Style and **Shape** Trough-shaped containers are well suited to areas of the garden above eye-level such as ledges on the tops of walls or terraces, so the plants can trail down the front edge of the planter. Other site suggestions include using tin trough plantings as window boxes so you can enjoy them from indoors and out. Or make up a series of matching troughs down a set of wide steps to soften harsh lines and allow both flowers and fragrance to spill over from step to step.

Size Height 18cm (7in); Width 60cm (24in).

Material Galvanised metal.

Salvia splendens 'Purple' See p.180

Verbena 'Diamond Merci'　　　　　See p.185

Verbena Tapien Violet　　　　　See p.184

Viola 'Bowles' Black'　　　　　See p.185

Fresh lime greens

Simply put, a limited colour palette and well-conceived structure, equals harmony and balance.

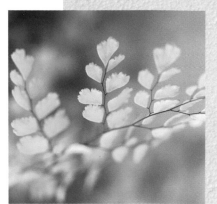
Adiantum capillus-veneris See p.157

INGREDIENTS	QTY
Adiantum capillus-veneris	× 5
Cordyline australis	× 1
Eucomis bicolor	× 5
Nicotiana 'Lime Green'	× 10

There is great artistic satisfaction to be had from experimenting with plants and pots, and in creating a display that combines shape, colour, texture, style and plant interest by using a very limited yellow-green colour palette. This unusual contemporary planting offers a great diversity of plant material from the spiky leaves of Cordyline through the broad smooth leaves of Eucomis to the soft and feathery fronds of the *Adiatum capillus-veneris* (Maidenhair fern). It carefully brings together a restful colour scheme with very deliberate contrasts of leaf shape and texture to give it extra appeal.

Cordyline australis See p. 164

PLANTING DETAILS

Planting plan This display is designed to be viewed from all sides. The key structural plants are the lone Cordyline – plant it first in the middle; and the five Eucomis – they go in next and are planted towards the rim and spaced evenly around the pot circumference. Plant two Nicotiana between each of the Eucomis. Tuck the ferns around the rim wherever space allows. The Eucomis and Nicotiana are small and then grow to scale but the Adiantum (Maidenhair fern) and Cordyline need to planted at a mature size because they will only put on a small amount of growth.

Plant care Deadhead the Nicotiana regularly to keep the planting looking its best.

Eucomis bicolor See p.168

CONTAINER DETAILS

Style and **Shape** This is a large-scale container in a subtle shade of khaki green with a glossy glazed ceramic finish. The plants have been carefully chosen so they do not detract from its mellow colour and simplicity. The container is tall, so to prevent the plant elements from looking squat, I have introduced a Cordyline in the centre to add height. On reflection, a slightly taller Cordyline might have been even better.

Size Height 75cm (30in); Diameter 60cm (24in).

Material Glazed ceramic.

Nicotiana 'Lime Green' See p.175

Modern rural

A vivid-coloured pot offers an interesting challenge which I have met with contrasting and vibrant plants.

INGREDIENTS	QTY
Hakonechloa macra 'Aureola'	× 4
Petunia 'Million Bells' Red	× 4
Petunia 'Million Bells' Cherry	× 4
Vinca minor 'Illumination'	× 4

Sometimes the colour and surface texture of the container cannot be ignored and should be allowed to lead the planting design. Here I have selected lime-green and vivid red and deep pink plant colours to draw out the pink and purple tones in the dumpy-shaped glazed ceramic pot. I enjoy using identical plants that have a close but subtly different colour relationship. Here I have used two types of Petunia hybrid, one in vivid red and one in deep pink and set these against variegated lime-green Vinca leaves and Hakonechloa grass. It makes the viewer look twice at the common Petunia and adds an extra dimension that might go unnoticed by some but will raise a wry smile from others.

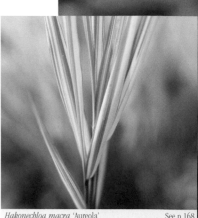

Hakonechloa macra 'Aureola'   See p.168

Petunia 'Million Bells' Red   See p.178

PLANTING DETAILS

Planting plan I used one large Hakonechloa plant that I split into four smaller plants by cutting the roots with a sharp knife and pulling them apart. The Vinca is then planted, evenly spaced, around the edge of the pot and then – as space in the pot is tight – I arranged the Petunias in amongst the Vinca and Hakonechloa – anywhere in fact there is room to spare.

Plant care Compared to the more common *Vinca minor*, this variegated type is slow growing. To encourage faster growth, buy the plants early in the season and give them a head start in a warm, well-ventilated greenhouse.

Petunia 'Million Bells' Cherry   See p.178

CONTAINER DETAILS

Style and **Shape** This low display is small enough to sit on a garden table or plinth outdoors. The flowers and foliage are both small in scale and match the proportions of each other and the ceramic pot. *Petunia* 'Million Bells' is far less vigorous than the more common *Petunia* Surfinia and, to my mind, has greater charm. Its blue-red petals pick up the colouring of the glazed ceramic, while the lime-yellow grass and leaves introduce a citrus note. The pale blue flowers of Vinca that appear late in the season detract from the pink and lime colour scheme so I prefer to remove them.

Size Height 35cm (14in); Width 40cm (16in).

Material Glazed and crazed ceramic.

Vinca minor 'Illumination'   See p.184

Setting standards

Simple shapes, sparse planting, and sympathetic colours give rise to restful and enduring displays.

Bacopa 'White Suttis 98'   See p.161

INGREDIENTS *in each container*	QTY
Bacopa 'White Suttis 98'	× 4
Isotoma (Laurentia) axillaris	× 2
Solanum rantonnetii	× 1

When looking at a group of containers, the eye is usually satisfied by symmetry and balance even if the matches are not exact. Reflected patterns and repeated themes or styles all help to create a reassuring sense of stablity. In this display, symmetry is achieved using a standard Solanum plant in each pot with the same quantity of Bacopa and Isotoma plants around the base of each "tree". Both plantings have been installed in similar but not identical pots manufactured from dark grey terrazzo. The slight variation in pot height and shape creates an intriguing imbalance that works to emphasise the symmetry of the plant material rather than disturb it.

PLANTING DETAILS

Planting plan This is an extremely simple planting that achieves its effect from the colour and lushness of the Solanums and the fragile look of their slender stems. Each Solanum was planted in the centre of its pot and given the extra support of a stout garden cane. The Bacopa was arranged around the rim and the two Isotoma plants were placed in between the Solanum and the Bacopas on the front edge.

Plant care Solanums need regular pinching out to keep their shape and maintain their flowering density. Two full growing seasons would produce standard Solanums of this size. Deadhead the Isotomas to keep them looking tidy.

Isotoma (Laurentia) axillaris   See p.172

CONTAINER DETAILS

Style and **Shape** The taller pot is a cylinder and the shorter one a square but the material is the same. This difference in shape is enough to set each apart but not enough for them to be seen as separate pieces that do not work together as a pair. Grey has a neutral tone that mixes with many colours but seems particularly suited to blue and purple flower colours.

Size Height 90cm (36in); Diameter 40cm (16in) *(tall cylinder)*.
Height 60cm (24in); Width 40cm (16in) *(square container)*.

Material Grey terrazzo.

Solanum rantonnetii   See p.181

Climbers and trailers

*A flowery mix in cool colours makes a delightful
small planting for the doorstep or patio.*

INGREDIENTS	QTY
Antirrhinum 'Trailing White'	× 2
Petunia 'Prism Sunshine'	× 2
Petunia 'White'	× 2
Senecio macroglossus 'Variegatus'	× 3
Thunbergia alata	× 1

In my experience, a lot of flowers can be packed into a small container and displays grown in these conditions are often subject to the kind of care and attention that simply would not be practical for plants grown in larger gardens. With regular feeding, watering, and deadheading the display will keep flowering for five months or more. I always try to make the best use of the pot space by growing climbers and trailing plants that thrive in these conditions such as Thunbergia (Black-eyed Susan) and *Senecio macroglossus* 'Variegatus'. I actively encourage the plants to spill out from the pot and go beyond to create a relaxed, informal arrangement.

Antirrhinum 'Trailing White'　　　　See p.158

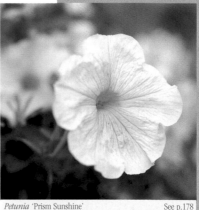

Petunia 'Prism Sunshine'　　　　See p.178

PLANTING DETAILS

Planting plan The arrangement was first created without Thunbergia (Black-eyed Susan). It was added later when the outdoor temperature had warmed up. A wigwam of sticks was put in at the start. The sticks could have been taller which would have meant less winding round and pinching out of the Thunbergia shoot tips but it did mean that many shoots wove their way in and through the other plants putting out bright orange flowers where they were least expected. The Senecio is vigorous and scrambled up the sticks as well as trailing over the rim of the pot. The Antirrhinum flowers come and go in quick bursts of flower throughout the season.

Petunia 'White'　　　　See p.179

CONTAINER DETAILS

Style and **Shape** This dumpy terracotta pot needs both height and trailing stems over its surface to make it appear more elegant. The Thunbergia (Black-eyed Susan) gives the display height and the Senecio adds long, trailing stems. As the season progresses the pot can be raised up to allow the Senecio to trail down further and balance the height of the climbing Thunbergia.
Size Height 28cm (11in); Diameter 30cm (12in).
Material Machine-made terracotta.

Senecio macroglossus 'Variegatus'　　　　See p.180

Thunbergia alata   See p.183

Desert modern

*A pure white trough and succulents that will tolerate
hot, dry conditions are ideal for exposed sites.*

INGREDIENTS	QTY
Echeveria glauca	× 3
Ophiopogon planiscapus 'Nigrescens'	× 8

This contemporary planting combines nothing more than the well-defined leaf shapes of grey-green Echeveria rosettes with the thin black strands of Ophiopogon grass. Both work together to complement the smooth, clean, rounded shape and white surface of this special trough cast from a mould of white composite resin. I enjoy working with a mix of just two plant types; when carefully chosen there is no confusion about the message they send out and they can make a much bolder statement than more complex arrangements. Also, the simpler the planting scheme then the more likely it is that the container will get noticed and here the great shape, style and material of this simple trough are shown off to full effect.

PLANTING DETAILS

Planting plan First, the three Echeveria rosettes were planted into the trough. Next, four Ophiopogon grasses were split in half to produce smaller tufts that could be tucked in between and around the rosettes. Any potting compost spilled into the centre of the Echeveria was blown out as its abrasive action will rub away the beautiful blue-grey bloom from the leaves of these succulents.
Plant care In hard-water areas, try not to spill water on the Echeveria because it will leave behind a noticeable white residue of lime. For the sake of tidiness, I like to remove the small lilac flowers of the Ophiopogon that appear late in the season.

Echeveria glauca   See p.167

CONTAINER DETAILS

Style and **Shape** Black and blue-grey foliage make natural colour partners and the contrasting leaf shapes show off each other to best advantage. The long plain container accentuates the shapely nature of the planting. Nature throws a spanner in the works by giving the Echeveria pink and yellow flowers – two colours that bear no relation to each other – they are the exception that proves the rule and I think that they add a quirky touch so I choose to leave them alone.
Size Height 18cm (8in); Length 75cm (30in).
Material White composite resin.

Ophiopogon planiscapus 'Nigrescens'   See p.174

Pale and hardy

Clean lines, monochrome planting and simple pot design is a foolproof way to a stylish arrangement.

INGREDIENTS *in rectangular planter*	QTY
Helichrysum italicum	× 3
INGREDIENTS *in tall cylinder*	QTY
Anthemis punctata subsp. *cupaniana*	× 1
Convolvulus cneorum	× 1

This collection of hardy plants favours a sunny position and the two containers and three plant species have been chosen to create a modern, fairly minimal design. This is achieved by using just two flower colours – white and yellow – and silver foliage. While the foliage in each planting offers variation in leaf shape, the tonal similarity helps keep the whole planting calm. The light pots are plain and regular. The plants are all perennials and evergreen so with regular feeding and a small amount of deadheading and trimming these container plantings will provide a permanent display, spanning several growing seasons.

Helichrysum italicum   See p.170

PLANTING DETAILS

Planting plan I planted the Convolvulus towards the back of the circular pot to allow the Anthemis room to spread out and so prevent overcrowding. I then planted three Helichrysums in the trough, following a symmetrical line down the centre.
Plant care As the Anthemis matures, flowers will spill down the face of the tall pot. Deadhead the flowers regularly to keep the planting tidy and to encourage more flowers after the first early summer flush. Cut back the Helichrysum (Curry plant) flowers as soon as they start to lose their colour. Make sure that the pots can drain freely as all these plants need well-drained conditions to stay healthy.

Anthemis punctata subsp. *cupaniana*   See p.158

CONTAINER DETAILS

Style and **Shape** Long, narrow troughs, like long, narrow garden flower borders, create a linear effect as there is no front-to-back dynamic. My advice is to keep the design simple and repeat one theme along its length. Here, I have used three curry-scented Helichrysums to do the trick and added a tall cylinder to break the horizontal; even though I think the trough would hold its own if it stood alone. I have also placed a white stone mulch on the soil surfaces to make the plantings appear even brighter.
Size Height 40cm (16in); Width 60cm (24in) *(rectangular planter)*.
Height 60cm (24in); Diameter 35cm (14in) *(tall cylinder)*.
Material White terrazzo.

Convolvulus cneorum   See p.164

Pillar-box red

Red is a passionate colour and, love it or hate it, a pillar-box red pot and planting cannot be ignored.

INGREDIENTS	QTY
Pelargonium 'Bushfire'	× 6
Pelargonium 'Ignescens'	× 2
Pelargonium 'Sassy Dark Red'	× 2
Sphaeralcea 'Newleaze Coral'	× 1

When planning a garden border, try limiting yourself to one flower colour. This will makes decisions much easier because it drastically reduces the number of plants to choose from.

Exactly the same rules apply – except on a smaller scale – when planting up a pot so if you want to make the design process realtively straightforward, choose plants in just one colour. It is made even easier if, like here, you have a bright pillar-box-red pot that is showing you the way. For maximum impact I have chosen vivid red petal colours. Subtle tones would also work but lack the immediate impact of these bold hues.

PLANTING DETAILS

Planting plan Pelargoniums provide some of the best and most intense reds and can be guaranteed to put on a good display throughout the summer months if the planter is kept in a sunny position.

Plant care Deadhead the pelargoniums regularly for continuous flowering throughout the summer and to maintain a tidy-looking display. Sphaeralcea is a straggly plant and its stems need support. I have pushed some twigs into the soil at the back of the pot and, as the stems develop, I will tie them onto the twigs to keep them in check.

Pelargonium 'Bushfire' See p.176

CONTAINER DETAILS

Style and **Shape** This tall columnar pot could almost be placed in the garden, unplanted, like a striking piece of modern sculpture. Pots like this are both an inspiration and a challenge. It holds a good quantity of potting mix though there is no need to fill it completely. To help keep the weight down, use a lightweight filler material (*see page 138*) and then a 40cm (16in) depth of potting compost on top.

Size Height 1m (40in); Width 36cm (14in).

Material Red-sprayed steel.

Pelargonium 'Ignescens' See p.177

Pelargonium 'Sassy Dark Red'   See p.177

Sphaeralcea 'Newleaze Coral'   See p.183

Purple haze

Two very different plants with similar flowers provide the link that holds this frothy planting together.

INGREDIENTS	QTY
Alyogyne huegelii	× 1
Lotus hirsutus	× 4
Petunia 'Blue Trailing'	× 4
Solenostemon 'Black Prince'	× 4
Viola 'Bowles' Black'	× 4

As many of my container plantings demonstrate, I enjoy large, bold foliage but I also like to experiment with smaller, less distinct foliage that relies on some characteristic other than its size or architectural shape to create an impression. Here I have chosen to use *Lotus hirsutus* which has small, downy grey leaves and a sufficiently tangled way of growing. It looks as if it is bearing the flowers of the Petunia – though, in reality, it has soft, pink-tinged flowers of its own. The Petunia and Alyogyne flowers run from top to bottom of the scheme to bring it all together.

Alyogyne huegelii   See p.159

Lotus hirsutus   See p.173

PLANTING DETAILS

Planting plan The Alyogyne foliage is finely cut and tends to get lost amongst the Lotus so a dark barrier of Solenostemon is planted between the two. In displays, I am always undecided as to whether I should leave the Solenostemon flowers intact or cut them off. In this case, their light blue colour does not cause offence so they remain. The Alyogyne is planted in the middle of the display with the Solenostemon plants in front and behind. The Lotus are put on either side to increase the width of the planting and so as not to overwhelm the Petunias that are planted in between. The small Violas fit in any leftover space and create dark areas amongst the foliage.

Petunia 'Blue Trailing'   See p.177

CONTAINER DETAILS

Style and **Shape** The container is a very simple, chunky, terracotta pot and when viewed from above it disappears under a soft grey frilly skirt and a flourish of blue Petunias. Rightly so. It is the plants and the detail they carry that are important here, not the pot. One concern was that the reddish-brown seedpods of the Lotus which appear in autumn would conflict with the purple and violet colour scheme but this was not the case and the planting continued to look good until late in the year.
Size Height 37cm (15in); Diameter 48cm (19in).
Material Terracotta.

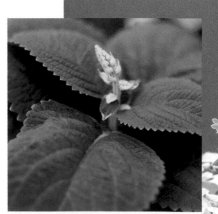
Solenostemon 'Black Prince'   See p.182

Viola 'Bowles' Black' See p.185

Quiet sophistication

Green is a calm and soothing colour and well-suited to this sophisticated planting for shady spots.

INGREDIENTS	QTY
Asparagus densiflorus	× 1
Aspidistra elatior	× 3
Carex morrowii 'Fisher's Form'	× 2
Tellima grandiflora 'Forest Frost'	× 2

This is a very clever mix of green foliage textures using four well-behaved plants that stay looking remarkably fresh with the minimum of effort. The display uses a diverse mix of foliage to create an arrangement that is both calming because of its colour but also visually exciting because of the mixture of shapes on offer. Here, the leaves have been carefully selected so that they range from the very frothy Asparagus fern to the broad and paddle-like Aspidistra, and from the flat and rounded Tellima leaves to the narrow and grass-like strands of Carex.

Asparagus densiflorus   See p.159

Aspidistra elatior   See p.160

PLANTING DETAILS

Planting plan There is a mix of hardy and tender plants being used here. The hardy plants, Tellima and Carex, are evergreen (the Tellima takes on reddish tints in the winter) and they can be left in the planter and enjoyed all year round.

Plant care The Aspidistra and Asparagus need to be lifted out and given indoor protection for the winter. The hole they leave in the planter could be filled with a green form of *Phormium tenax* or a small *Phormium cookianum* 'Tricolor'. Both species would provide good alternative winter interest.

Carex morrowii 'Fisher's Form'   See p.164

CONTAINER DETAILS

Style and **Shape** This Versailles planter has a simple and classic shape that lends itself particularly well to the formal and symmetrical style of this display. Square planters are ideal for arrangements that have a definite front view and the flat rear side will sit up against the garden wall.

Size Height 45cm (18in); Width 45cm (18in).

Material Softwood planter, painted dark green.

Tellima grandiflora 'Forest Frost'   See p.182

Exotic explosion

When mixing tender and hardy plants, try to make sure that they have some characteristics in common.

INGREDIENTS	QTY
Cordyline australis 'Torbay Red'	× 1
Helichrysum petiolare 'Limelight'	× 4
Osteospermum jucundum	× 4

Cordyline australis 'Torbay Red'   See p.165

In this display, a close visual link is made between the exotic appearance of the hardy *Osteospermum jucundum* and the more tender Cordyline and Helichrysum leaves. The showy flowers of the Osteospermum betray its South African origin and help define its exuberant personality. These flowers sit cheerfully alongside the spiky red Cordyline leaves and the lime-green Helichrysum foliage. As the whole planting matures, the Osteospermum flowers and Helichrysum foliage will spill over the edge of the container. This will make the pot appear less dominant and create a better visual balance, with the tall Cordyline in the centre.

PLANTING DETAILS

Planting plan A square pot is a good shape for a container gardener as the space available inside makes planting-up straightforward. Place the Cordyline in the centre, one Osteospermum plant in each corner and each of the four Helichrysums between the Osteospermums along each face of the pot. If the arrangement is only seen from one side, leave out the Helichrysum from the back of the display to allow more space for the roots of the other plants to grow.

Plant care In a sheltered site, both Cordyline and Osteospermum are likely to survive the winter. The Helichrysum will not, and is really only a summer addition.

Helichrysum petiolare 'Limelight'   See p.170

CONTAINER DETAILS

Style and **Shape** Cordylines do not increase in size very much during a single season so choose a plant that balances the scale of the pot. The colours of the Cordyline and Osteospermum have been chosen to complement each other and to contrast in colour and texture with the Helichrysum foliage. The silvery grey pot offers a neutral background to lay the flowers and leaves over. Place this planting at the end of a view along a path or through a gateway. Equally, it could take centre stage in a small courtyard garden.

Size Height 48cm (19in); Width 45cm (18in).

Material Glazed frost-resistant ceramic with a grey, semi-matt finish.

Osteospermum jucundum   See p.175

Bright grasses

Strong foliage is the backbone of a successful planting design either in the garden or in a container.

INGREDIENTS *in small container*	QTY
Carex oshimensis 'Evergold'	× 2
Carex phyllocephala 'Sparkler'	× 1
Lamium galeobdolon 'Hermann's Pride'	× 4
INGREDIENTS *in large container*	QTY
Hakonechloa macra	× 3
Liriope muscari 'Variegata'	× 2
Phormium tenax 'Variegatum'	× 1

To my mind, variegated foliage plants are not always very easy to place in the garden; their coloured foliage often looks too exotic to fit in easily, whereas in a container – where we are often expecting the exotic – they look more at home. Strong foliage looks particularly effective when several variegated plants are used in combination, as shown here.

In this grouping, the light green and white colour of the foliage has been picked up by the clever choice of pots. The soft yellow flowers of the Lamium are yet to come but will reflect the colour of the lime-green ceramic glaze seen on the smaller pot.

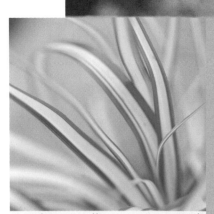
Carex oshimensis 'Evergold'   See p.163

Carex phyllocephala 'Sparkler'   See p.163

Lamium galeobdolon 'Hermann's Pride'   See p.172

PLANTING DETAILS

Planting plan The large pot is planted with the Phormium at the back so that the planting has a front. The smaller pot is planted with its tallest plant in the middle so that it can be viewed from all-round.

Plant care This planting uses hardy plants and *Carex oshimensis* 'Evergold', Liriope, and Phormium are reliably evergreen. Though others are herbaceous, and will die back in winter, a reasonable display can be expected throughout the year with little maintenance. In a mild winter, *Carex phyllocephala* 'Sparkler' and Lamium will also keep their leaves.

CONTAINER DETAILS

Style and **Shape** Using pots in pairs offers extra scope for creating a more interesting display. The pot colour can be used to enhance the planting but also to play off the pots against each other. The difference in pot height is another element that the container gardener can exploit. All the variables of tall and short plantings with high and low containers heights should be considered.

Size Height 20cm (8in); Width 80cm (32in) *(tall pot)*.
Height 37cm (15in); Diameter 40cm (16in) *(small pot)*.

Material Frostproof glazed ceramic.

Hakonechloa macra   See p.168

Liriope muscari 'Variegata'   See p.173

Phormium tenax 'Variegatum'   See p.178

Sunshine colours

This is a lively, fizzy arrangement where flowers play a major role and foliage provides background "mist".

INGREDIENTS	QTY
Abutilon 'Kentish Belle'	× 1
Antirrhinum Luminaire ™ 'Deep Trailing Yellow'	× 4
Bidens ferufolia 'Golden Star'	× 4
Petunia 'Prism Sunshine'	× 4

The large Petunia flowers and the leaves of the Abutilon are the only elements of any size, and the scheme's effectiveness relies upon the flowers sitting in a frothy tangle of fine and feathery foliage. To create the sunny feel I have used various shades of yellow enriched by the red "cups" (calyces) of the Abutilon, which are also picked up by the reddish buds of the Antirrhinum. The tangle of Bidens and trailing Antirrhinum is self-supporting, but the arching Abutilon stems benefit from some twiggy support to prevent them from falling over as they get longer and heavier with flowers. But leave some Abutilon flowers to flop over into the planting, providing additional colour to the body of the display.

PLANTING DETAILS

Planting plan In this lively, sun-loving combination, the tall billowy plants explode from the dark, solid pot like an erupting volcano. The effect is intensified here with sparks of fiery yellow and red that resemble molten lava. The Antirrhinum flowers tend to come in bursts throughout the season, providing a constant see-saw of anticipation and satisfaction.

Plant care Deadhead the Petunias as they go over to prevent the spent flowers lying on and rotting the other plants. Some pinching out of the Bidens will be necessary if it is not going to overwhelm everything else.

CONTAINER DETAILS

Style and **Shape** The container is a deep steely blue, square metal box – its flat surfaces provide an excellent foil for the flowers and feathery foliage and its solidity makes the planting look even more delicate. Its large size and capacity allow a good front-to-back depth of planting to create rich and abundant arrangements.

Size Height 50cm (20in); Width 50cm (20in).

Material Lightweight metal with a double skin and a coated surface.

Abutilon 'Kentish Belle' See p.157

Antirrhinum Luminaire ™ 'Deep Trailing Yellow' See p.158

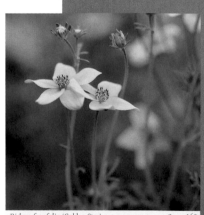

Bidens ferufolia 'Golden Star' See p.162

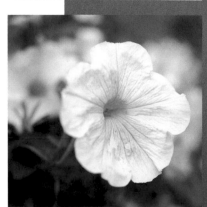

Petunia 'Prism Sunshine' See p.178

Textured grey-greens

Soft grey-greens and browns are often undervalued but for subtle, textured displays, they are unbeatable.

INGREDIENTS *in large container*	QTY
Cussonia paniculata	× 1

INGREDIENTS *in small container*	QTY
Dichondra 'Silver Falls'	× 2
Kalanchoe tomentosum	× 1

Just three species are on show in this planting, and all of them grey, but their differences in leaf shape and habit turn what could be a dismal scheme into something unique that generates considerable power and dynamism. The textural qualities of the plants begs close-up inspection, not just for visual delight but also for the tactile experience. Dichondra has silky smooth leaves and stems, Kalanchoe has a stiff velvet feel – its brown-edged leaves creating a visual link with the terracotta pots – and the deeply lobed Cussonia foliage is both smooth and leathery.

Cussonia paniculata

See p.167

Dichondra 'Silver Falls'

See p.166

Kalanchoe tomentosum

See p.173

PLANTING DETAILS

Planting plan This simple planting requires no specific planting instructions but the key is to find the right site free from distracting colours or conflicting textures that are likely to disturb its simplicity.

Plant care To maintain the planting in good health requires little work. The plant that needs most attention is the Dichondra, as its shoots have a tendency to overwhelm the Kalanchoe. To prevent this, trim off shoots as and when required.

CONTAINER DETAILS

Style and **Shape** These elliptical-shaped large and small terracotta pots are hand-decorated with the same pattern of short grey scratches. They could not be more perfect for this grey-themed design. The "teardrop" shape of both pots offers plenty of width for planting but is narrow enough from front to back to stand close to the wall for maximum effect.

Size Height 60cm (24in); Width 60cm (24in) *(large container).*
Height 40cm (16in); Diameter 35cm (14in) *(small container).*

Material Patterned frostproof terracotta.

Silver selection

A structured jumble of plants can create lots of visual excitement in a pot without appearing chaotic.

INGREDIENTS	QTY
Dichondra 'Silver Falls'	× 3
Elymus magellicanus	× 1
Hebe pimeliodes 'Quicksilver'	× 3
Kleinia senecioides	× 1
Plectranthus argentatus	× 1
Plectranthus cilatus	× 3

This is a glorious all-in mix of textures and shapes within a grey and silver theme. There is not a flower to be seen but still the eye is led this way and that, skipping from smooth to furry from silky to succulent and from fleshy to filigree. Even when the eye is satisfied the sense of touch is still in a state of excitement. Run your fingers round the smooth pot for a tactile experience before starting on the numerous plant surfaces. Begin the experience with the pink velvet-like stems of *Plectranthus argentatus*.

Dichondra 'Silver Falls' See p.166

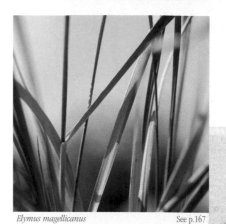
Elymus magellicanus See p.167

PLANTING DETAILS

Planting plan Sadly, the tall centre stems of the *Plectranthus argentatus* which gave the display its height were damaged and had to be taken out. But their removal exposed the beautiful silvery Elymus grass behind and prevented the Plectranthus from dominating the design. Perhaps, in future, I will be more deliberately ruthless.

Plant care This planting contains a mix of hardy and tender plants. At the end of the season remove the hardy Hebe and Elymus. Pot them up and leave them outside until next year, or plant them out in the garden until you need them. If you wish to keep the tender plants, pot them up and over-winter them in a heated greenhouse.

CONTAINER DETAILS

Style and **Shape** There are so many ingredients in this planting that it is something of a relief that the pot itself is very smooth surfaced and a simple, round-bottomed shape; a complete contrast to the frenzied plant-growing activity going on inside.

Size Height 60cm (24in); Diameter 40cm (16in).

Material Grey composite.

Hebe pimeliodes 'Quicksilver'   See p.169

Kleinia senecioides   See p.173

Plectranthus argentatus   See p.179

Plectranthus cilatus   See p.179

Spiky partners

An effective way to show off an enthusiastic collection of succulents is in a bold, simple grouping.

INGREDIENTS *in centre-front container*	QTY
Aeonium arboreum	× 2
INGREDIENTS *in left container*	QTY
Agave americana 'Variegata'	× 1
INGREDIENTS *in centre-back container*	QTY
Aloe ferox	× 1
INGREDIENTS *in right container*	QTY
Opuntia lindheimeri	× 1

Just because you collect plants of a certain genus or type does not mean that you have to treat them like precious gems and hide them away. Almost all species of plants can be shown off in well-chosen stylish containers that enhance the plants and the collection. Cacti and succulents are particularly suited to display because of their architectural shapes. Here they are planted in a mixed selection of large and small, galvanised and stainless-steel planters. Both the durability and grey colour of these metals works well with cacti and succulents; plants that are well-known for their endurance and heat-tolerant nature.

Aeonium arboreum See p.157

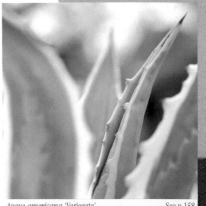

Agave americana 'Variegata' See p.158

Aloe ferox See p.159

PLANTING DETAILS

Planting plan The spiky plants need careful handling. Wear thick leather gloves when planting up the Opuntia. To protect your eyes from the sharp leaf tips of the Agave, push corks onto the leaf points or wear goggles as an extra precaution. The Opuntia and Aeonium, in particular, will benefit from being grown in these heavy, and therefore stable, metal pots, particularly as they start to grow bigger and become more and more top heavy.

Plant care All these plants need good drainage and plenty of sun to thrive.

CONTAINER DETAILS

Style and **Shape** Both galvanised and stainless-steel need no maintenance. Brand new galvanised metal will lose some of its brightness as the surface oxidises but stainless-steel retains its shiny finish.

Size Height 42cm (17in); Width 42cm (17in) *(left cube)*.
Height 30cm (12in); Length 60cm (24in) *(narrow trough)*.
Height 100cm (40in); Width 40cm (16in) *(centre-back cylinder)*.
Height 40cm (16in); Width 36cm (14in) *(right pot)*.
Material Galavanised metal and stainless-steel.

Opuntia lindheimeri See p.174

Rambling rhodochiton

Height is often difficult to achieve in containers but introducing a climber can solve this problem.

INGREDIENTS	QTY
Cerinthe major 'Purpurascens'	× 2
Plectranthus zatarhendii	× 1
Rhodochiton atrosanguineus	× 1

In my experience of tall container designs, it is best to try and achieve a ratio of about one third pot to two-thirds climber for a balanced look. Climbing plants in pots will need support. For a natural look, I like to use branches cut from trees or shrubs in the garden rather than buying bamboo canes at a garden centre. Not only are the curves and bends of the branches more elegant but, on a practical level, the plants' cling more readily to their rough surface. Hazel shoots are a good choice because they are both straight and flexible and make ideal supports for climbing plants in pots. Simply push three hazel shoots into a pot, and tie the tips together just below the tops to create a "tepee-style" structure.

Cerinthe major 'Purpurascens'   See p.165

PLANTING DETAILS

Planting plan The three Hazel poles span the soil surface. A single Rhodochiton plant at the foot of one of the poles and allow new shoots to climb up all three. The Cerinthe sits in the middle of the pot using the poles for support as it grows. Like a trailing version of *Plectranthus argentatus*, *P. zatarhendii* spills its velvet-grey foliage over the pot edge. Once it reaches the ground, it is likely to root and provide a quantity of rooted cuttings for other container plantings next year.

Plant care Cerinthe and Rhodochiton produce prolific quantities of seed. Save some at the end of the season to grow next year's plants.

Plectranthus zatarhendii   See p.180

CONTAINER DETAILS

Style and **Shape** This simple planting is inspired by the colour and shape of the pot. The glazed pot has a smooth silky finish: a marvellous foil for the velvet Plectranthus leaves. Its dumpy but upright style is ideal for tall plantings because the relatively broad base helps to stabilise the arrangement while the eye is carried upwards to take in the plants.

Size Height 55cm (22in); Diameter 45cm (18in).

Material Glazed ceramic.

Rhodochiton atrosanguineus See p.180

Intensely modern

Plants that are exhibitionists and shout out, "Look at me" are often the ones that work well in containers.

INGREDIENTS	QTY
Canna 'Pretoria'	× 3
Cordyline australis Purpurea Group	× 4
Cuphea 'Tiny Mice'	× 3
Uncinia rubra	× 1

This fabulous planting is an excuse to show off the extraordinary leaves and rich orange flowers of Canna 'Pretoria' and to create some exotic and colourful excitement just for its own sake. The small Cuphea flowers are such an intense red that they sit like red hot embers in a hearth. They appear to be waiting to be fanned into life in order to set ablaze the grassy leaves of Uncinia and Cordyline, and also to release the flaming orange flowers of the Canna. The tall pot shape helps to raise up the plants to eye level to further increase their dramatic visual impact.

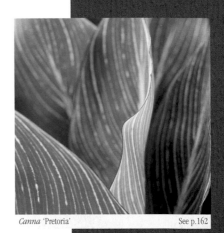

Canna 'Pretoria' See p.162

PLANTING DETAILS

Planting plan This display shows how simple it is to bring together plants in a range of different sizes in one pot to create a full display. I often use a large Cordyline plant as the central feature in a pot, (*see pages 28-29*) but here I bought some small Cordyline plants that are ideal for tucking in amongst other busy foliage to add some contrasting spiky structure. Potted on, the Cordyline will grow into big plants for future use but here they do a perfect job of filling in between the Cannas at the back of the planting and the Cupheas at the front. As a bonus the colour of the Cordyline leaves matches the rust-coloured pot surface perfectly.

Cordyline australis Purpurea Group See p.165

CONTAINER DETAILS

Style and **Shape** The rust-effect coated steel container has a textured shiny finish that adds to the sparkle and vigour of the planting. Its height and width are ideal to balance the spread of the wide Canna leaves, which have more growing to do as they exploit the generous amount of potting compost this large container can hold.
Size Height 60cm (24in); Width 42cm (17in).
Material Rust-effect coated steel.

Cuphea 'Tiny Mice'   See p.166

Uncinia rubra   See p.184

Regal red and gold

The wind gives life to this planting, as it gently buffets the flowers and swirls the grasses about.

Carex buchananii   See p.164

INGREDIENTS	QTY
Carex buchananii	× 1
Osteospermum 'Serena'	× 3
Persicaria microcephala	× 3
Solenostemon hybrid	× 3

Plants are sensitive to changes in light and temperature, and different weather conditions can alter the plant's appearance on a day-to-day or even minute-by-minute basis. This planting was photographed on a sunny but windy day. As the wind picked up you could catch a glimpse of the wonderful russet colours on the reverse side of petals. On calmer, sunnier days, the apricot-pink Osteospermum flowers are content to open out fully and shine upwards from a rich bed of orange and brown foliage, hiding their undersides until the sun goes down and the petals close up, revealing the dark rust beneath.

Osteospermum 'Serena'   See p.175

PLANTING DETAILS

Planting plan This arrangement is designed to be seen from just one side, even though it is planted up in a round container. The grass is planted at the back of the display (rather than in the middle) and every other ingredient is placed in front of the grass to create a forward-facing display.

Plant care This display is a mix of low-maintenance plants that grow up to form a dome-shaped planting. Pinch out the pale blue flowers of Solenostemon (Coleus) so that they do not spoil the fiery red colour effect of the foliage. Also, pinch out the growing tips of the Persicaria leaves to control their height and so maintain shape.

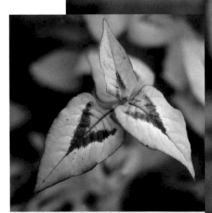

Persicaria microcephala   See p.176

CONTAINER DETAILS

Style and **Shape** The half-egg shape of the grey terrazzo pot lends itself to this slightly squat, dome-shaped arrangement, which says, "I am not wild and flamboyant but I am offering you subtle textures and tones of browns and green if you just take the trouble to look."

Size Height 35cm (14in); Width 40cm (16in).

Material Grey terrazzo.

Solenostemon hybrid   See p.182

Metallic hues

Hardy, all-year-round plantings can be as exciting and stylish as more exotic summer plantings.

INGREDIENTS *in small container*	QTY
Heuchera 'Silver Scrolls'	× 1

INGREDIENTS *in large container*	QTY
Carex buchananii	× 3
Carex comans 'Frosted Curls'	× 2
Heuchera 'Silver Scrolls'	× 2
Phormium tenax	× 1

INGREDIENTS *in medium container*	QTY
Carex buchananii	× 2
Convolvulus cneorum	× 1
Ophiopogon planiscapus 'Nigrescens'	× 2

There are very few winter-flowering plants suitable for containers but that does not mean a winter display has to be dreary. These three pots rely entirely on leaf colour and shape for their winter effect. For a seasonal change during the summer months, the Heucheras throw up spikes of flower and the Convolvulus sports open white blooms. In a sheltered site, the Heuchera flowers will last into autumn.

Carex buchananii See p.164

Carex comans 'Frosted Curls' See p.163

PLANTING DETAILS

Planting plan The same principles apply to winter plantings as to summer displays; tall plants at the back with a gradual decrease in scale to the front edge. In the two larger pots, *Phormium tenax* and *Carex buchananii* add height but offer very different styles. Heucheras and Convolvulus fill the foreground. In the largest pot the long tresses of *Carex comans* 'Frosted Curls' spill over to the floor.

Plant care Plants put on very little growth during the winter so when planting specifically for winter effect, buy mature plants to get the desired result.

Convolvulus cneorum See p.164

CONTAINER DETAILS

Style and **Shape** Because of the limited range of plants available for winter displays the containers themselves play an important part. A matching set of three pots sets the style of the design, and their textured metallic surfaces look great when thrown into relief by the shadows cast by the winter sun.

Size Height 64cm (26in); Width 64cm (26in) *(large)*.
Height 38cm (15in); Width 38cm (15in) *(medium)*.
Height 29cm (12in); Width 29cm (12in) *(small)*.
Material Coated terracotta.

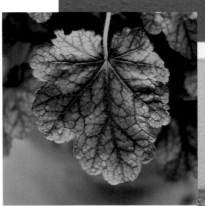

Heuchera 'Silver Scrolls' See p.171

Ophiopogon planiscapus 'Nigrescens'   See p.174

Phormium tenax   See p.178

Mellow apricots

This warm display blends apricots, oranges and browns to produce a sumptuous late summer palette.

INGREDIENTS	QTY
Carex flagellifera 'Coca-cola'	× 3
Lotus maculatus	× 4
Mimulus aurantiacus	× 1
Osteospermum 'Serena'	× 3
Viola 'Apricot'	× 3

This amorphous tangle of flowers and wispy filaments of grass blends together an array of warm gentle flower and foliage colours to provide an overall mellowness that evokes not autumn but summer evenings when the sun is all but set and its warmth still radiates from the walls and ground. Each flower has a distinct style of its own and, for this reason, no single plant dominates the display. This adds to the relaxed, informal nature of the arrangement and this becomes even more so as the season progresses and the plants start spilling over the edges of the terracotta pot.

Carex flagellifera 'Coca-cola'   See p.164

Lotus maculatus   See p.174

PLANTING DETAILS

Planting plan *Mimulus aurantiacus* does not know whether it wants to grow upwards or sprawl sideways so I have let it do both. I have tied some upright shoots to twiggy supports pushed into the middle of the planting and let other shoots spread over the edge of the pot. The Lotus struggled to establish itself and would probably have been better off without so much competition.

Plant care Osteospermums need regular dead-heading to keep the planting tidy but, more importantly, to ensure a continuous supply of new flowers.

Mimulus aurantiacus   See p.175

CONTAINER DETAILS

Style and **Shape** There are a lot of plants in this display and they need plenty of compost in order to stay healthy. Fortunately, this wide almost straight-sided pot has plenty of capacity for potting compost. The rich terracotta colour of the pot is ideally suited to the warm colours of the planting.

Size Height 50cm (20in); Diameter 60cm (24in).

Material Handmade, frostproof terracotta.

Osteospermum 'Serena'   See p.175

Viola 'Apricot'   See p.184

Moody reds

An eruption of sultry red plant material blows out of this large cone with all the drama of a volcano.

INGREDIENTS	QTY
Canna 'Black Knight'	× 3
Dahlia 'Ragged Robin'	× 1
Impatiens 'Accent Cranberry'	× 4
Imperata cylindrica 'Rubra'	× 5

Rich deep red flower and foliage colours are successfully brought together to create a feeling of fiery sumptuousness and at the same time a moody sense of foreboding. Here purple-tinged and flame-red foliage are added to a mix of crimson and red flowers to produce a pot full of glowing embers almost waiting to be fanned into flame by the breeze. Using contrasting foliage shapes and textures adds further to the excitement as each vies for attention. The large leaves of the Canna provide a solid background for the frothy Dahlia leaves while the grassy foliage of Imperata jump like spark trails from the heart of the fire.

Canna 'Black Knight'
See p.163

Dahlia 'Ragged Robin'
See p.166

Impatiens 'Accent Cranberry'
See p.170

Imperata cylindrica 'Rubra'
See p.171

PLANTING DETAILS

Planting plan Plant up the display from the back to the front of the container. Start with the Cannas, then plant the Dahlias, the Imperatas and lastly the Impatiens (Busy lizzies) in the foreground. At first the design will lack balance as the Dahlia plants grow faster than the Canna but, as the season progresses, it will fill out as planned.

Plant care Use a fertile potting compost and create good drainage to make it possible to grow this mix of plants together (normally they have different cultural requirements to one another). Water and feed the plant material regularly to keep it healthy. Deadhead the Dahlias to encourage the plants to keep flowering.

CONTAINER DETAILS

Style and **Shape** This large galvanised steel cone offers the perfect shape and material for creating a dramatic and moody container display. The conical shape has the effect of thrusting the abundant plant material upward and outward. Combine it with dark sultry flower and foliage colours and you have a potent and evocative mix.

Size Height 77cm (31in); Diameter 60cm (24in).

Material Galvanised steel.

Ivy topiary

Tough and reliable container plantings that stay looking good from year to year, are to be treasured.

INGREDIENTS *in each container*	QTY
Athyrium filix-femina 'Frizelliae'	× 2
Athyrium niponicum var. *pictum*	× 3
Hedera helix 'Amber Waves'	× 3
Hedera helix 'Lalla Rookh'	× 1

Ivy plants tend to be overlooked by the experienced and amateur gardener alike because they are widespread. But with a little imagination, this ubiquitous plant can be grown in pots to create low-maintenance, durable, and stylish displays. Here to counter the formal style of the topiary ivy "lollipops" each terracotta pot is underplanted with the textured leaves of ferns and a different decorative variety of ivy to add botanical interest as well as a bit of frill. The ferns also provide some seasonal change to the appearance of the display as they die back in winter and then shoot up again in spring.

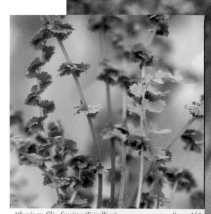
Athyrium filix-femina 'Frizelliae' See p.160

Athyrium niponicum var. *pictum* See p.160

PLANTING DETAILS

Planting plan To create an ivy topiary, take a bushy ivy plant and remove all the trailing stems except for the two longest. Remove all the leaves but retain the last few at the end of each shoot. Plant it at the base of a strong plastic tube pushed well into the potting compost. Wire an upturned hanging basket to the top of the tube. Twist the bare stems in opposite directions around the plastic tube and tie with twine where they cross. Trim out side shoots as the main shoots grow upwards. When the shoots reach the basket, weave them through the holes to form a full head of ivy.
Plant care Trim off any wayward shoots to keep the ball-shaped heads compact.

Hedera helix 'Amber Waves' See p.169

CONTAINER DETAILS

Style and **Shape** I have chosen simple terracotta pots to counteract the busy planting. Because it is a permanent display, I have used straight-sided pots that hold as much potting compost as possible. Also, the wide pot bases help to prevent these top-heavy trees from blowing over in high winds.
Size Height 26cm (10in); Width 50cm (20in) *(two identical containers)*.
Material Terracotta.

Hedera helix 'Lalla Rookh' See p.169

Solid structures

Carefully chosen plants and distinctive containers combine to create a warm but modern look.

INGREDIENTS *in small planter*	QTY
Askiodiosperma paniculatum	× 1
INGREDIENTS *in medium planter*	QTY
Calopsis paniculata	× 2
INGREDIENTS *in large planter*	QTY
Chondropetalum mucronatum	× 2

Containers made from wood have a nautral affinity with plants. They will survive quite happily outdoors and many wooden planters actually improve with age as their surface becomes weathered. Wooden planters are often associated with traditional or country styles of garden but solid wood planters in simple designs can produce plantings for the most contemporary garden setting. Here, I have chosen simple wood container shapes and used only a limited range of evergreen plants, selected because they belong to the same family. It is an understated and restful plant combination – all the more restful because it requires little aftercare.

Askiodiosperma paniculatum — See p.159

Calopsis paniculata — See p.163

PLANTING DETAILS

Planting plan All three plants belong to the family *Restionaceae*, members of which are usually known as Restios. They grow best in acid soil. To make life easier, plant just one species per container so that you do not have to worry about satisfying the needs of several different types of plant in one place. A group of three planters also gives you the opportunity to arrange each one so that it looks its best. I chose these Restios for their obvious architectural strengths, their evergreen nature and the brownish colour of their bracts that ties the planting to the colour of the wood.
Plant care Water the plants with soft water to maintain soil acidity.

CONTAINER DETAILS

Style and **Shape** These "Versailles-gone-modern" planters offer the enduring appeal of traditional wooden tubs but with a smarter, modern edge. They come fitted with a metal liner to help protect the wooden outer casing from soil moisture but also to make it easier to repot or transplant whatever is growing inside.
Size Height 43cm (18in); Width 43cm (18in) *(small planter)*.
Height 52cm (21in); Width 52cm (21in) *(medium planter)*.
Height 71cm (28in); Width 71cm (28in) *(large planter)*.
Material Solid oak.

Chondropetalum mucronatum — See p.164

Shades of purple

Begonias are well-known as houseplants but will enjoy a summer holiday outdoors in containers.

INGREDIENTS *in container on ground*	QTY
Begonia 'Connie Boswell'	× 1
Begonia 'Fireworks'	× 1
Begonia 'Solid Silver'	× 1
Tradescantia pallida 'Purpurea'	× 1

INGREDIENTS *in trough on wall*	QTY
Begonia 'Martin Johnson'	× 1
Begonia 'Peace'	× 2
Ipoemoea batatas 'Blackie'	× 1

In my experience, popular houseplants like Tradescantia, Chlorophytum (Spider plant), Solenostemon (Coleus) and Begonias that are used to languishing indoors on a windowsill for most of the year, take on a new lease of life when given the opportunity to grow outdoors during the summer months. Here, Tradescantia and a selection of ornamental Begonias form the foundation of this trough and tub display. The plants grow so well outdoors when given a good depth of soil and favourable growing conditions that they become almost unrecognisable from the indoor specimens.

Begonia 'Connie Boswell' See p.161

Begonia 'Fireworks' See p.160

PLANTING DETAILS

Plant care Usually, I grow all the plants in my container displays in a loam-based potting compost but for Begonias I use a peat-based compost, which they prefer. These very ornamental Begonias can take a surprising amount of direct sunlight but too much heat can make the leaves lose their distinctive colouring and lustrous leaf gloss. Begonias are best grown in a well-lit position but out of direct sunlight. These conditions will also suit the other plants in the display. If well-fed and watered Begonia varieties like 'Peace' and 'Solid Silver', will produce spectacularly big leaves.

Begonia 'Solid Silver' See p.161

CONTAINER DETAILS

Style and **Shape** I have used two different metal containers to complement the metallic sheen of the Begonia leaves. The trough has a smooth, galvanised steel finish while the tub is an old recycled copper cistern rescued from a scrapyard. They make a good pair but will also work equally well on their own.
Size Height 20cm (8in); Width 80cm (32in) *(trough)*.
Height 37cm (15in); Diameter 40cm (16in) *(pot on ground)*.
Material Galvanised steel trough and recycled copper tub.

Tradescantia pallida 'Purpurea' See p.184

Begonia 'Martin Johnson'   See p.161

Begonia 'Peace'   See p.161

Ipoemoea batatas 'Blackie'   See p.171

Low-maintenance pink

Although this mauve-pink Osteospermum looks rather exotic, it is in fact a hardy plant.

Heuchera 'Plum Pudding' See p.171

INGREDIENTS	QTY
Heuchera 'Plum Pudding'	× 1
Osteospermum jucundum	× 4

The hardy nature and evergreen foliage of *Osteospermum jucundum* are very useful assets to the gardener. Its beauty lies in the fact that it can be set up in a container and left outside all year round. When the warmer weather comes, the Osteospermum produces long-stemmed daisy-like flowers that will bloom from late spring to autumn. The Heuchera is equally low-maintenance with its foliage providing year-round interest and then, in summer, it throws up tall spikes of tiny flowers. A row of pots along a path edge or sunny wall using this Osteospermum and Heuchera mix will provide good year-round interest with the minimum of cost or maintenance – very effective and very simple.

Osteospermum jucundum See p.175

PLANTING DETAILS

Planting plan This is simplicity itself. Plant the Heuchera in the centre of the pot and equally space the four Osteospermums around it. Once established, the Osteospermums will spread out quickly to fill the spaces in between.

Plant care Here are two self-sufficient plants that need little looking after. Plant both the Osteospermum and Heuchera in a loam-based potting compost and make sure that they are fed regularly throughout the growing season. Shelter the pot from cold winds so that the Heuchera foliage does not become wind-scorched.

CONTAINER DETAILS

Style and **Shape** Long-term plantings need a large volume of potting compost to stay healthy. Straight-sided pots hold the maximum amount of soil for a given diameter but this slightly flared pot offers both a visually pleasing shape and a generous interior space for plant growth. The container's silky black finish complements the dark plum Heuchera leaves.

Size Height 40cm (16in); Diameter 45cm (18in).

Material Black glazed ceramic.

Textured trail

Low, wide containers are a useful addition to the courtyard garden and they look great in paved areas.

Asparagus densiflorus See p.159

INGREDIENTS	QTY
Asparagus densiflorus	× 4
Pelargonium 'Lady Plymouth'	× 4
Plectranthus madagascariensis Variegated mintleaf	× 4
Senecio petasitis	× 1

Low plantings sit on the ground – well below eye-level – which makes them ideal for placing in front of garden ornaments, like statuary, as they will not interrupt your line of vision. Low container plantings can also work well when placed near a favourite garden bench or in front of a group of taller containers where they will have the effect of spreading and enriching all the other container-grown material. In most cases, the style of the pot is not really important because it will not be seen. The low arrangement will be looked down on, and a full and healthy planting will have filled out and trailed over the edges of the container well before the end of the season.

PLANTING DETAILS

Planting plan The pot is planted up in a classic configuration, with the tall Senecio planted in the centre of the display and three concentric circles of different foliage plants around it. This arrangement relies on the fresh green tones of variegated leaves and will thrive in light shade.

Plant care As the season progresses the Senecio will get taller but if you pinch out the growing tips early on it will fill out and become bushier. Encourage the Plectranthus to trail across the paving with the occasional strand running back into and through the feathery Asparagus fronds and the large Senecio leaves.

CONTAINER DETAILS

Style and **Shape** The main drawback of using a shallow container is that it holds a smaller volume of potting compost than a deeper pot. This may limit the plants' potential growth. When choosing a low container, try to find one that has a wide diameter – as seen here – to compensate for the shallow depth.

Size Height 30cm (12in); Diameter 70cm (28in).

Material Terracotta.

Pelargonium 'Lady Plymouth'   See p.177

Plectranthus madagascariensis Var'd mintleaf   See p.179

Senecio petasitis   See p.181

Flame colours

Orange is a colour avoided by many gardeners but why and for what reasons it is hard to understand.

INGREDIENTS	QTY
Begonia fuchsiodes	× 4
Canna musifolia	× 2
Canna Orange hybrid	× 2
Crocosmia 'Star of the East'	× 2
Isoplexis canariensis	× 1
Pelargonium tormetosum	× 1

I find that the trick with using orange flowers successfully in planting schemes is to mix them in with plenty of greenery so that they do not overpower the arrangement. I also try to mix up pure orange flowers with other shades of orange and closely associated vibrant reds. This jam-packed collection of lush foliage produces a well-balanced effect. Here, the green foliage is more dominant and the orange flowers peer out from between the leaves but without their fire, I think that the arrangement would fall flat.

Begonia fuchsiodes See p.162

Canna musifolia See p.162

PLANTING DETAILS

Planting plan *Canna musifolia* is planted across the back edge of this square pot. I split a large clump into several small pieces and strung them out in a line so that their huge leaves provide a solid backdrop to the planting scheme. The Isoplexis is planted in the pot centre for height and it is grown as a standard on a clear stem. The *Begonia fuchsioides* are planted around the base of the Isoplexis on each side with the short Canna hybrids planted at the front edge. The soft-leaved Pelargonium then sits between these Canna hybrids.

Plant care This lush planting needs plenty of water and weekly feeding to sustain it.

Canna Orange Hybrid See p.162

CONTAINER DETAILS

Style and **Shape** This is the sort of container shape that I enjoy. Its scale is big, so I can use large plants and get plenty of front-to-back depth in the planting. It has a great volume which I can fill with plenty of potting compost to support the amount of growth I expect. Lastly, the container surface carries the minimum of decoration so it does not detract from the beauty of the plants.

Size Height 60cm (24in); Width 65cm (26in).

Material Plastic imitation of terracotta.

Crocosmia 'Star of the East' See p.165

Isoplexis canariensis   See p.171

Pelargonium tormetosum   See p.176

Shade-loving foliage

Strong foliage shapes in fresh minty greens and whites add a bright note to a shady corner of the garden.

INGREDIENTS *in left container*	QTY
Aegopodium podagraria 'Variegatum'	× 1
INGREDIENTS *in centre-back container*	QTY
Petasitis japonicus 'Nishiki-buki'	× 1
INGREDIENTS *in right container*	QTY
Tolmeia menziesii 'Taff's Gold'	× 3

There are certain plants that have an invasive nature and no matter how attractive they look you need to be very wary of letting them loose in your garden. Growing them in the confines of a pot is the ideal solution as it enables you to enjoy them without fear they will overwhelm your other garden plants. In this arrangement both Aegopodium and Petasites are invasive but they have very good-looking foliage that is fabulous when grown in containers alongside Tolmeia. All three plants will do well in a shady part of the garden where flowery plants would struggle to perform.

Aegopodium podagraria 'Variegatum'   See p.157

PLANTING DETAILS

Planting plan With just one plant species in each pot, planting is extremely easy. To cover the pot more quickly, split the single Aegopodium plant into several smaller parts. All three are hungry plants so add some controlled-release fertiliser to each of their potting composts before planting.

Plant care These hardy perennials can be left in their pots all-year-round, although they will die back in winter. They will benefit from regular feeding and should be repotted after two or three years – be careful where you discard any unwanted pieces of Petasites plant material, they are likely to root themselves and spread.

CONTAINER DETAILS

Style and **Shape** This is a low planting and when viewed from above the pots are barely visible. I have used three plain black glazed pots. They are slightly different in shape and size to give some interest when the plants die back in the winter.

Size Height 23cm (9in); Diameter 37cm (15in) *(left)*.
Height 34cm (14in); Diameter 38cm (16in) *(centre)*.
Height 38cm (16in); Width 33cm (13in) *(right)*.

Material Glazed ceramic.

Petasitis japonicus 'Nishiki-buki'
See p.177

Tolmeia menziesii 'Taff's Gold'
See p.183

Bright and bold

Don't shy away from brightly coloured containers, use them to inspire bold and modern planting schemes.

INGREDIENTS	QTY
Geranium 'Ann Folkhard'	× 2
Penstemon 'Blackbird'	× 1
Salvia farinacea 'Victoria'	× 4
Tibouchina urvilleana	× 1

This vivid-blue metal container has an intensity of colour that is difficult to match in nature. However, I decided to rise to the challenge and find vivid-coloured flowers that would hold their own when forming an alliance with this intense blue partner. Tibouchina, Geranium, and Penstemon in shades of purple and magenta work well because they have enough blue in their colour make-up to link them to the pot as well as red tones to help them stand out. Purple Salvias are also good allies because their flowers contain a mixture of blue and red hues.

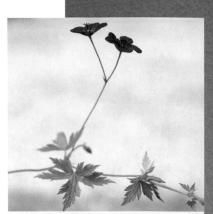
Geranium 'Ann Folkhard'   See p.169

Penstemon 'Blackbird'   See p.176

PLANTING DETAILS

Planting plan Tibouchina is central to this arrangement and usually produces a mass of large, very showy purple flowers but my two plants refused to flower. *Salvia farinacea,* planted in front of the Tibouchina, performed well as did the lime-green leaved *Geranium* 'Anne Folkard' planted along the front edge of this square pot. Later in the season, the old leaves of Tibouchina turn bright orange before they drop off. If you do not wish to upset the carefully controlled balance you may find these leaves disturbing; here, I saw it as an advantage because it helped to spice up the display.
Plant care Train the vigorous Geranium shoots away from the centre of the planting.

Salvia farinacea 'Victoria'   See p.181

CONTAINER DETAILS

Style and **Shape** The bowed sides of this square container give it a slightly dumpy appearance. To slim down the pot shape, it helps to grow trailing plants over the sides. I have used the hardy *Geranium* 'Anne Folkard' but it is very vigorous and will need to be thinned out as the season progresses if the pot is to remain visible.
Size Height 60cm (24in); Width 44cm (18in).
Material Powder-coated steel.

Tibouchina urvilleana   See p.183

Luscious leaves

Matching a pot to a plant is container gardening at its simplest but, potentially, most powerful.

INGREDIENT *in left container*	QTY
Begonia 'Contesse de Montesquieu'	× 3
INGREDIENT *in centre container*	QTY
Solenostemon 'Juliet Quartermain'	× 1
INGREDIENT *in right container*	QTY
Begonia 'Fire Flush'	× 3

A group of three separate containers each planted up with a different but well-chosen leafy plant can offer an attractive alternative to a mixed planting. Each separate element also has flexibility because it can be moved about or repositioned against a suitable background colour or texture to reinforce the overall design. This style of display will also satisfy the keen plant collector who wants to be able to enjoy the distinctive character of the plant's attributes in isolation, without compromising the group dynamic; for a gardener, to grow plants in this controlled way surely offers the best of both worlds.

Begonia 'Contesse de Montesquieu' See p.160

PLANTING DETAILS

Plant care Growing just one species per pot means that you do not have to concern yourself with plant compatibility or creating the best conditions to make every species happy. You can simply provide the one plant with the conditions it needs to grow well. In this grouping, I found that the two pots that hold the Begonias have rims that turn inwards, making it difficult to lift out the established Begonia plants to re-pot them. To make the Begonia plants easier to move when mature, first plant them into a smaller plastic pot, to contain their roots, and then place the plastic pot inside the ceramic one.

CONTAINER DETAILS

Style and **Shape** This arrangement uses a subtle rust colour palette but for added interest the pots are slightly different in colour and have very different finishes. The two Begonia pots have a stony matt surface and the tall cylinder, a glossy ceramic glaze – a difference not big enough to upset the planting but enough to make you look again.
Size Height 36cm (14in); Width 36cm (14in) *(left and right)*.
Height 42cm (17in); Diameter 36cm (14in) *(centre)*.
Material Stone composite (left and right) and glazed ceramic (centre).

Solenostemon 'Juliet Quartermain'   See p.183

Begonia 'Fire Flush'   See p.160

Rusty hues

I like to liven up permanent plantings by throwing one or two colourful plants into the mix in summer.

INGREDIENTS	QTY
Carex flagellifera 'Coca-cola'	× 4
Crocosmia 'Star of the East'	× 3
Cuphea ignea	× 1
Thunbergia alata	× 1

My garden flower borders benefit from the addition of tender plants in the warm summer months, and I like to treat my permanent container plantings in the same way, choosing colours and styles of flower that will enhance the more established residents. First, the display has to be tidied up to make room for some fresh potting compost and the tender Cuphea and Thunbergia plants. This means cutting back the wispy Carex grass and cutting out some of the deep Crocosmia roots. Fortunately, most plants are able to withstand a certain amount of root damage, especially when they are actively growing. I find that the serrated blade of a bread knife is the ideal tool for cutting out these tough roots.

Carex flagellifera 'Coca-cola' See p.164

Crocosmia 'Star of the East' See p.165

PLANTING DETAILS

Planting plan This simple-looking planting needs a certain amount of pre-planning. The hardy Carex grasses form the backbone of the planting and are beautiful in their own right but to add some late-season colour Crocosmia corms were planted into the pot the previous autumn. Their flowers range in colour from soft yellow to intense red and they make very good hardy container plants. Prior to flowering, Crocosmias will also provide good green foliage. Thunbergia and Cuphea are tender and are should be planted in late spring when the weather improves and the chance of frost has passed.

Cuphea ignea See p.166

CONTAINER DETAILS

Style and **Shape** This square, reeded pot was chosen so that its straight lines and formal look would set off the informal, fluffy character of the Carex grass. The pot also contributes a certain amount of style and interest during the winter months when only the grass is showing. Also its pinkish terracotta colouring is well suited to the earthy brown and orange tones that characterise this display.
Size Height 50cm (20in); Width 40cm (16in).
Material Plastic imitation terracotta.

Thunbergia alata See p.183

Bluegrass Melody

Large-scale plantings in huge pots are as impressive as garden sculpture – go big, bold and dramatic.

INGREDIENTS	QTY
Argyranthemum foeniculaceum	× 4
Ceropegia linearis subsp. *woodii*	× 6
Leymus arenarius	× 3
Helichrysum petiolare	× 4
Melianthus major	× 1

There is plenty of room in this large but lightweight square metal container, which provides an exciting opportunity to create a dramatic large-scale arrangement. The scale and size of the container actually demand an extravagant planting style with a head-turning selection of leaf shapes and textures. Also, the sheer volume of potting compost that it can hold, means that all five plants will have enough space and nutrients to achieve healthy and vigorous growth. The flamboyant display will suit a range of garden locations but, wherever it is placed, it is asking to be the centre of attention and should be given a prominent position where it can stand alone.

Argyranthemum foeniculaceum　　　See p.159

Ceropegia linearis subsp. *woodii*　　　See p.165

PLANTING DETAILS

Planting plan The huge metal pot and the large grey-leaved Melianthus were the inspiration for the whole planting scheme, which follows a grey/white colour note. The dramatic planting includes the vigorous blue-grey grass *Leymus arenarius*. This is an invasive plant but safe when grown in the confines of a pot. *Helichrysum petiolare* – another vigorous plant – was also chosen for its silvery leaves, Argyranthemum to add some highlights of white, and Ceropegia to contribute some interesting leaf detail and to help cover the sides of the pot. All the foliage was planted from the centre out, and evenly spaced around the Melianthus plant in the middle of the pot.

Helichrysum petiolare　　　See p.170

CONTAINER DETAILS

Style and **Shape** At 90cm (36in) high and 60cm (24in) square, the container is big and looks big, so it is important to use plants like Ceropegia that trail over the sides and visually reduce the container's bulk. Despite its solid appearance, the planter is made from a double skin of thin metal so it is lighter than it looks. When planted up, it is only half-filled with potting compost to help keep down its overall weight.
Size Height 90cm (36in); Width 60cm (24in).
Material Twin-walled, zinc-coated metal.

Leymus arenarius　　　See p.173

Melianthus major   See p.174

Contemporary display

Take note: flowers can be temperamental and may not always perform, but good foliage is always reliable.

Carex flagellifera 'Coca-cola' See p.164

INGREDIENTS	QTY
Carex flagellifera 'Coca-cola'	× 3
Dahlia 'Bednall Beauty'	× 3
Kleinia senecioides	× 1
Salvia 'Raspberry Royale'	× 2

I chose this variety of Dahlia because of its ability to produce an abundant display of very deep red flowers over a sustained period and because it has beautiful dark feathery foliage.

However, when I planted up the trough the Dahlias produced flower buds but they refused to open. The idea behind this planting scheme was to produce an arrangement that provides layers of contrast of texture and shape. In theory, the Dahlia and Salvia flowers appear together with a similar colour and intensity and tie the planting together. The succulent, *Kleinia senecioides* (Senecio) is added for its texture and to break up the mass of the dark Dahlia foliage and soften the front edge of the container.

PLANTING DETAILS

Plant care To encourage the Dahlias to spill forward over the edge of the metallic trough, I pinched out the tips to a forward facing bud when the plants were young. As these shoots become heavier and grow towards the light they naturally lean forward. Later in the season the Carex puts out grassy flowers on long stalks adding a more graceful and softer look to the display. The foliage of *Kleinia senecioides* (Senecio) will also spill over and reach the ground well before the end of the season. Deadheading the Dahlia flowers is also important for maintaining a succession of flowers.

CONTAINER DETAILS

Style and **Shape** Troughs of this size and capacity are ideal for creating full, dense plantings. They work well when arranged in groups in contemporary courtyard areas where a square or geometric look is all important. Troughs provide a good length of display without projecting too far forward, making them the perfect shape for a narrow walkway or anywhere space is limited.
Size Height 40cm (16in); Width 85cm (34in).
Material Powder-coated steel.

Dahlia 'Bednall Beauty'　　　　　See p.167

Kleinia senecioides　　　　　See p.173

Salvia 'Raspberry Royale'　　　　　See p.181

Lemon layer cake

*I call this style of display an "aromatic layer cake"
to be enjoyed in a shady corner of a warm garden.*

INGREDIENTS	QTY
Alocasia sanderiana	× 5
Fatsia japonica	× 1
Pelargonium 'Lady Plymouth'	× 5

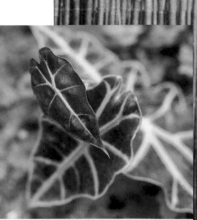

Alocasia sanderiana See p.159

Aromatic citrus scents are usually associated with the sun-loving foliage of Mediterranean shrubs but here I have chosen the delicious eucalyptus and lemon fragrance of *Pelargonium* 'Lady Plymouth' which favours half shade. This Pelargonium not only smells wonderful but produces attractive variegated green leaves. Sitting above the Pelargoniums are the large white-veined leaves of Alocasia. They need more warmth than most English summers can provide to reach their full size but the leaf shapes offer a welcome contrast to the glistening Fatsia foliage above and to the variegated Pelargonium leaves below.

PLANTING DETAILS

Planting plan This domed display is designed to be seen from all sides and is very simple to plant up. The Fatsia sits in the centre, the Pelargoniums are evenly spaced around the rim. The Alocasias fill in the gaps between.

Plant care Take care not to let the Pelargonium foliage overwhelm the Alocasia. The flowers on *P.* 'Lady Plymouth' are small and pink. In my opinion, they spoil the leafy green effect and should be pinched off periodically.

CONTAINER DETAILS

Style and **Shape** Here is a gloriously rotund, white crackle glazed pot with enough of a hint of blue to cool the white almost to ice. Too cold, I thought at first, but as the Alocasia leaves developed they carried the blue tones into the planting, lessening the cold effect. Ceramic pots of these dimensions are heavy and, once planted up, are difficult to move. Choose a place for the pot and position it before planting.

Size Height 50cm (20in); Width 60cm (24in).

Material White glazed ceramic.

Fatsia japonica   See p.169

Pelargonium 'Lady Plymouth'   See p.177

container
materials

Container choice

*Available in a host of new and traditional materials,
the choice of outdoor containers has never been better.*

The upsurge in small-space living and a desire for instant results has renewed people's interest in container gardening. This, in turn, has led to huge innovations in pot design and use of materials from which they are made. Traditional container materials like terracotta and stone are being used to create modern adventurous designs, while experiments with new materials like moulded resin have given rise to an unprecedented choice of planters. There is now a style, shape, size and colour of pot for every gardening situation and, if what you want doesn't exist, a one-off planter or group of planters can be commissioned at an affordable rate. Such variety of containers gives ample scope for innovation and indulgence.

WHICH MATERIAL IS BEST?

There are a mixture of both practical and aesthetic decisions to be made when selecting the best container for your needs. Wooden containers have a natural appeal but unless they are made from the more expensive hardwoods, like oak, they will need regular maintenance to prevent them from deteriorating in the wet.

Like wood, terracotta has a natural affinity with all plant material and looks good when teamed up with most plant combinations. But terracotta is porous and dries out more quickly so plants in terracotta pots need frequent watering.

Metal containers create a clean, pared down contemporary look and their hard surfaces are easy to clean. Terrazzo and some synthetic planters create the same visual effect as metal with their simple designs. There are also now some very good synthetic copies of lead cisterns and large terracotta pots which can achieve a grand effect on a budget.

	ADVANTAGES	DISADVANTAGES

Clay

A common and versatile material suitable for a variety of garden styles. It is available as traditional terracotta or with a glaze applied to the surface in a wide range of colours and finishes.

- Unglazed terracotta is porous and therefore plant-friendly. It carries air to the plant roots.
- Unglazed terracotta takes emulsion paint giving you an unlimited colour range.
- Clay pots are heavy and so bring stability to large or top-heavy plantings.

- Unglazed terracotta absorbs water from the potting compost so the plants need watering more frequently.
- If water seeps in beneath the glaze, the pot is prone to frost damage.
- Clay pots are likely to break if they are dropped or accidentally topple over.

Wood

The only container material that is a renewable resource. Natural wood planters available in soft- and hardwoods are unobtrusive and blend well with plant material.

- Wood is easy to work and light to handle making it ideal for producing your own plant containers at home.
- It is impervious to frost.
- Wood takes paints and stains so colours can be changed or refreshed each year.

- Wood planks can only be made into square or rectangular shapes so only a few designs are possible.
- Life is short, if the wood is untreated.
- Painted softwood needs regular maintenance to prevent it from rotting.

Stone

Though often regarded as a traditional material for classic-style urns, modern techniques have produced a host of exciting stone containers in contemporary shapes and styles.

- Non-porous so does not dry out the potting compost too quickly.
- Strong and durable.
- Stone compounds are readily moulded so there is a broad range of shapes and patterns from complex to plain and simple are available.

- All stone products are heavy which makes them very stable but often extremely difficult to move to another location without help.
- Stone containers can be expensive.

Metal

Originally, metal containers were often recycled utilitarian items like animal troughs and water cisterns. However, new ways of working with metal have led to more adventurous pot designs.

- Good choice of shapes, colours and finishes in old, recycled and new pots.
- Stylish designs available. Metal finishes are ideal for clean contemporary design.
- Frost-proof.

- Steel containers are prone to rust so choose products with quality coatings if you want your containers to last.
- May scratch or dent.
- Poorly galvanised products can have dangerously sharp or rough edges.

Synthetic

Made from plastics, polymers, fibreglass, and resins, synthetic containers are available in almost any colour, shape, texture or finish.

- Synthetic materials are usually tough but lightweight, making them suitable for roof terraces and balconies.
- Frost-proof.
- Fake stone, metal and terracotta pots in traditional designs are available at a fraction of the cost of the real thing.

- Abrasions and scuffs can cause permanent damage.
- Poor copies can look cheap and artificial.
- The pot surface does not age well or develop an attractive patina like containers made of natural materials.

Clay

This natural material can be hand-thrown on a potter's wheel, shaped in a mould, or built up in coils.

The beauty of natural clay is that its colour can vary from pale pink to deep rich reds and greys, depending on which region the clay has been extracted from. The best terracotta pots are handmade, and the only ones I avoid are those that have a very narrow neck because they can break in cold weather when the potting compost inside freezes and then expands as it thaws. Before the pots are fired in the kiln, the clay surface can be easily scored, pressed and patterned to provide a range of textures and finishes. They can be elaborately decorated with moulded swags and nymphs, or more simply decorated with latticework or a repeat pattern.

If you like this traditional material but want something that looks modern, buy clay pots that have been glazed in contemporary colours. In my view, single colour glazes are inspirational, while mixed colour glazes can be distracting and difficult to use in combination with plant material.

Terracotta is the ideal material for country-style plantings such as this. Within two or three seasons, this pale-surfaced pot will age beautifully, building up a rich patina of colour as a result of algal growth. The algae live on the crusted salts and nutrients that leach out through the porous terracotta surface from the potting compost when the planting is watered.

SOAKING TERRACOTTA BEFORE PLANTING

Terracotta pots are ideal containers for plants because they are porous and allow air to the roots but the natural porosity of this material also creates problems, especially for young plants. Dry terracotta pots will soak up any excess water from the potting compost and dry it out completely, depriving young plants of much-needed moisture. To help prevent the plants from drying out, give them an extra thorough watering before planting and also soak your empty terracotta in a bucket of water so that it is fully saturated with liquid.

LINING GLAZED POTS WITH PLASTIC

Glazed clay pots that have not been glazed on the inner surface and those with a crackle glaze finish are vulnerable to frost damage (*see page 148*) because water can seep in under the glaze. To prevent frost damage, line the insides with a layer of heavy-duty plastic sheeting to make them waterproof. Here, I have used blue polythene from a builder's merchant but clear, black or green polythene may be more suitable in a garden setting. Ensure that the lining has a generous overlap and extends down to the base of the pot without covering the drainage hole. This waterproof lining technique will also prevent salts from leaching through a crackle glaze finish and will ensure that the outer surface of the pot stays clean.

A selection of clay containers

Sizes are shown as *height x diameter*

1   Lime glazed clay pot; *37cm (15in) x 40cm (16in)*
2   Handthrown terracotta spiral; *35cm (14in) x 20cm (8in)*
3   Metallic painted terracotta ; *29cm (12in) x 29cm (12in)*
4   Flame red glazed ceramic; *37cm (15in) x 40cm (16in)*
5   Hand-finished terracotta; *10cm (4in) x 20cm (8in)*
6   Hand-thrown terracotta pot; *53cm (21in) x 45cm (18in)*
7   Hand-decorated terracotta; *40cm (16in) x 35cm (14in)*
8   Hand-decorated terracotta; *15cm (6in) x 30cm (12in)*

9   Mixed glazed ceramic; *35cm (14in) x 40cm (16in)*
10   Aubergine glazed pot; *53cm (21in) x 45cm (18in)*
11   Hand-thrown terracotta; *30cm (12in) x 45cm (18in)*
12   Grey glazed ceramic; *37cm (15in) x 40cm (16in)*
13   Dark blue glazed ceramic; *35cm (14in) x 25cm (10in)*
14   Latticework terracotta pot; *53cm (21in) x 45cm (18in)*
15   Pewter glazed terracotta; *60cm (24in) x 45cm (18in)*
16   Olive glazed terracotta; *75cm (30in) x 60cm (24in)*

17   Handthrown terracotta urn; *80cm (32in) x 60cm (24in)*
18   White crackle-glazed pot; *50cm (20in) x 60cm (24in)*
19   Black speckle-glazed pot; *45cm (18in) x 45cm (18in)*
20   Honey glazed pot; *37cm (15in) x 40cm (16in)*
21   Sage glazed pot; *53cm (21in) x 45cm (18in)*
22   Hand-thrown terracotta; *80cm (32in) x 80cm (32in)*
23   Slate grey glazed clay urn; *68cm (27in) x 35cm (14in)*

Wood

Containers made of wood make perfect partners for plants but need oil and preservative to extend their life.

Wood is an organic material and when it comes into direct contact with moist potting compost it will start to break down as a result of bacterial and fungal activity. Untreated softwood planters may only last up to a year but softwood that has been pressure-treated during manufacture will last between ten and fifteen years. To extend the pot life and prevent staining, some of the more expensive tubs and boxes come fitted with metal or plastic liners which are a very good idea.

In contrast to other materials like stone, terracotta, and metal, containers made from wood are cheap and easy to construct yourself at home with limited DIY skills. The advantage of this is that you can custom-build a container that will fit the space available, and be confident that it has the capacity for healthy plant growth. When the container is built you can finish it in almost any colour and style of decoration.

The wooden "Versailles-style" tub is a classic design well-suited to traditional and modern garden situations. To prolong the life of the container, empty it of plants and potting compost periodically and dry it out. Check the wood for signs of decay and treat the interior with a wood preservative.

PROTECTING WITH WOOD STAIN

Painted softwood containers are particularly susceptible to water damage at the joints and seams because they rarely have a chance to dry out completely once they have been planted up. To avoid wood rot, it is a good idea to paint wooden boxes with a coloured wood stain that contains preservative. Before you start, make sure that the wood is dry and sound. If the wood has already been pressure treated – by which I mean soaked with preservative under pressure by the timber supplier – then this extra coat will add even more protection. Always check that the preservative or paint you use is plant-friendly.

PROTECTING WOOD BY OILING

Untreated wood that is exposed to the sun will dry out and is prone to cracking. To limit this damage, feed the dry wood with linseed oil during the winter months when the box is clean and free of plant material. This linseed oil treatment will help preserve the wood and bring out the rich natural grain. Also. coat the interior with wood preservative to protect it when it comes into contact with the moist potting compost and extend its life.

A selection of wooden containers

Sizes are shown as *height x width*

1 Weathered pine trough; *20cm (8in) x 60cm (24in)*
2 Woven wicker basket; *25cm (10in) x 30cm (12in)*
3 Stained pine box; *42cm (17in) x 15cm (6in)*
4 Woven hazel basket; *20cm (8in) x 40cm (16in)*
5 Wooden barrel; *40cm (16in) x 45cm (18in)*
6 Wooden barrel; *40cm (16in) x 45cm (18in)*
7 Solid oak planter; *42cm (17in) x 42cm (17in)*
8 Stained wood box; *20cm (8in) x 10cm (4in)*
9 Teak outer liner; *57cm (23in) x 57cm (23in)*

10 Painted wood Versailles tub; *45cm (18in) x 45cm (18in)*
11 Solid oak planter with liner: *72cm (29in) x 72cm (29in)*
12 Weathered solid oak planter; *53cm (21in) x 53cm (21in)*
13 Blue wood-stained pine trough; *90cm (36in) x 30cm (12in)*

Stone

In container gardening, "stone" includes natural stone, terrazzo, concrete, and reconstructed stone.

Apart from natural stone which has to be cut by machine or carved by hand, garden containers made from other stone-based materials can be formed in a mould which allows for the mass production of many different sizes and shapes of pots at relatively low prices.

Reconstructed stone – which is simply stone "powder" bound with an adhesive – is used to make authentic-looking copies of traditional container shapes, like urns and pots mounted on pedestals. Some manufacturers in an attempt to make their new pots look old and weathered also use coloured additives and surface coatings in the production process. Many contemporary containers, however, are available in simple square or cylinder shapes and their appeal relies on the smooth matt surfaces and pale grey and white tones that reconstituted stone, concrete and terrazzo finishes have to offer.

The tactile surface of this container made from textured stone compound provides a good foil to the black leaf colour and smooth, fleshy feel of the Aeonium leaves.

AGEING STONE CONTAINERS

To achieve an aged appearance, you need to establish the growth of algae and lichens on the pot surface. New pots, particularly those in sunny sites, present a hostile environment for these organisms to establish themselves. To encourage algal growth, you need to supply nutrients for the organisms to grow. Simply rub a fistful of lush juicy grass across the pot surface. This green grass stain soon fades to brown. Other methods include brushing a layer of thinned natural yoghurt over the pot surface or spraying on a liquid fertiliser. When treated, place your pots in a damp shady site in long grass to create the ideal conditions for algae and lichens to flourish.

CLEANING STONE CONTAINERS

When planting up containers, it is easy to spill potting compost and leave behind dirty finger marks on the pale stone surface. Most marks can usually be rubbed off when dry or washed off using soapy water and a plastic kitchen scourer. For stubborn stains, try using a "Wet and Dry" abrasive pad which is used to rub down scratches on car body paint and is available from most large DIY stores. If in any doubt about the effect this abrasive action will have on a smooth stone pot surface, check the result on a hidden area first.

A selection of stone containers

Sizes are shown as *height x width*

1   Tobacco terrazzo pot; *35cm (14in) x 35cm (14in)*
2   Pale grey terrazzo cylinder: *35cm (14in) x 40cm (16in)*
3   Reconstituted stone bowl; *30cm (12in) x 40cm (16in)*
4   White terrazzo trough *25cm (10in) x 30cm (12in)*
5   Black terrazzo pot *36cm (14in) x 45cm (18in)*
6   White terrazzo cylinder; *60cm (24in) x 35cm (14in)*
7   White terrazzo cylinder; *60cm (24in x 20cm (8in)*
8   White terrazzo rectangle; *40cm (16in) x 60cm (36in)*
9   White terrazzo pot; *60cm (24in) x 60cm (24in)*

10   Candy twist concrete urn; *50cm (20in) x 40cm (16in)*
11   Stone pedestal urn; *45cm (18in) x 60cm (24in)*
12   Grey terrazzo cylinder; *90cm (36in) x 40cm (16in)*
13   Grey terrazzo trough: *35cm (14in) x 50cm (20in)*
14   Granite bowl; *20cm (8in) x 45cm (18in)*
15   White terrazzo square; *35cm (14in) x 35cm (14in)*

Metal

Casting, pressing, bending, and rolling are just some of the techniques used to make metal containers.

During manufacture, the surface of the metal can be treated by galvanising, painting, coloured-powder coating and polishing to create a number of different matt and reflective finishes. This huge choice of effects, makes metal a popular choice for the container gardener. Metal is also appealing because it is very durable and will survive outdoors with little or no maintenance. However, metal containers are not inert; galvanised surfaces will eventually lose their bright shiny look and turn grey as the zinc oxidises. Some steel containers, designed with a rust finish can cause staining on light paving stones. To prevent this staining, make sure that water can drain away from the pot base. Some gardeners avoid metal containers because they think that they conduct heat too efficiently, scorching the roots and drying out the potting compost but, in my experience, it never appears to have a harmful effect on the plants.

Powder-coated metal containers provide some of the most vivid-coloured pots available. Their brilliance is enhanced by their smooth, shiny finish and satisfying shapes. Some container manufacturers have stock colours and surface finishes and are also able to offer specific colours by special order.

PREVENTING RUST IN DRAINAGE HOLES

The big enemy of metal is rust. To protect against this, the manufacturers apply a zinc coating or galvanise the metal. Paint and powder coatings also offer protection. With all of these it is important not to damage the protective coating or the metal will corrode. However, sometimes plant containers are manufactured without drainage holes and you will need to drill holes into the pot base if the plants roots are to stay healthy. After drilling, reseal the broken metal surface with a protective coat of anti-rust paint. This will prevent the metal from rusting as water drains through the planting.

CLEANING POLISHED METAL CONTAINERS

Highly polished stainless steel or aluminium containers make a strong visual statement. To maintain the impact of their bright reflective surface, you will need to keep the surface highly polished, using a window-cleaning spray and a soft cloth. Do not use abrasive scourers as they will scratch the surface. When watering the plants, take care not to splash water or potting compost onto the polished metal. In hard water areas, these splashes will leave behind white deposits of calcium which can be rubbed off with a soft cloth. A regular application of a protective wax car polish repels water and makes polishing less hard work.

A selection of metal containers

Sizes are shown as *height × width*

1   Galvanised metal cylinder; *40cm (16in) × 30cm (12in)*
2   Galvanised metal vase; *37cm (15in) × 15cm (6in)*
3   Brushed stainless-steel; *50cm (20in) × 60cm (24in)*
4   Stainless-steel cube; *30cm (12in) × 30cm (12in)*
5   Recycled copper pot; *37cm (15in) × 40cm (16in)*
6   Stainless-steel pot; *40cm (16in) × 30cm (12in)*
7   Galvanised metal pot; *37cm (15in) × 15cm (6in)*
8   Recycled metal tub; *65cm (26in) × 40cm (16in)*

9   Rust-effect coated steel vase; *70cm (28in) × 42cm (17in)*
10   Galvanised metal bucket; *65cm (26in) × 60cm (24in)*
11   Blue powder-coated steel; *60cm (24in) × 44cm (18in)*
12   Red sprayed steel; *1m (40in) × 36cm (14in)*
13   Galvanised metal pot; *37cm (15in) × 40cm (16in)*
14   Twin-wall blued steel; *90cm (36in) × 60cm (24in)*
15   Recycled copper cylinder; *37cm (15in) × 20cm (8in)*
16   Aluminium pot; *1m (40in) × 40cm (16in)*

17   Galvanised metal cube; *45cm (18in) × 45cm (18in)*
18   Galvanised metal trough; *35cm (14in) × 90cm (36in)*
19   Lead planter; *40cm (16in) × 40cm (16in)*
20   Rust-effect coated steel; *60cm (24in) × 42cm (17in)*

Synthetic

This category includes fake lead and terracotta pots in traditonal designs and more radical resin planters.

One look at the selection of containers on display opposite shows you how versatile polymers, plastics, fibreglass and resins are and what creative and imitative use they can be put to in container design. Virtually any size or scale of container is now acheivable in curvy or straight shapes, in ridged, bobbly or smooth textures or in matt or shiny metallic finishes. What is so exciting for the container designer prepared to experiment with these new materials is that the method of manufacture rarely limits the shape or size of the container, and even large-scale planters are relatively lightweight and inexpensive to produce. For those who prefer more traditional styles, manufacturers of synthetic pots are also able to offer extremely convincing copies of traditional lead, terracotta and stone container shapes. The advantages of the synthetic versions is that they are cheaper as well as being frostproof and unbreakable.

Unlimited by the constraints of working with a natural material, shapes of all sorts can be made using synthetic materials and moulds. Here, a long trough has a wonderful rounded shape. Its clean and shapely lines are the perfect foil for the rosettes of the succulent.

CLEANING SYNTHETIC CONTAINERS

Potting compost stains and dirty hand prints can be easily removed from most synthetic materials with soapy water and a soft cloth. More stubborn marks may require the use of a kitchen scouring pad but try it out on a hidden area first if you are worried about damaging the surface. Take care to avoid scuffing or scratching plastic surfaces because once damaged there is no foolproof way of removing the marks.

LIGHTWEIGHT BENEFITS

A significant advantage of synthetic materials is their strength to weight ratio. The materials are tough but lightweight. For this reason, large pots are easy to transport to any location and they are easy to put away if you are not using them. There are some very convincing lightweight "rock" or "stone" containers that allow solid-looking pots and features to be used in places such as balconies roof gardens or on wooden deck areas where weight and how to carry the pot to the high-rise site are often an issue.

A selection of synthetic containers

Sizes are shown as *height × width*

1 Fake stone square; *25cm (10in) × 25cm (10in)*

2 Fake copper pot; *40cm (16in) × 30cm (12in)*

3 White moulded resin pot; *30cm (12in) × 33cm (13in)*

4 Fake lead square; *37cm (15in) × 37cm (15in)*

5 White moulded resin trough; *18cm (7in) × 75cm (30in)*

6 Blue plastic container; *37cm (15in) × 45cm (18in)*

7 Fake cast iron pot; *37cm (15in) × 50cm (20in)*

8 Orange moulded resin pot; *30cm (12in) × 33cm (13in)*

9 Fake lead trough; *20cm (8in) × 75cm (18in)*

10 Fake terracotta rectangle; *50cm (20in) × 40cm (16in)*

11 Grey moulded resin planter; *30cm (12in) × 45cm (18in)*

12 Fake lead tub; *45cm (18in) × 40cm (16in)*

13 Grey moulded resin planter; *45cm (18in) × 60cm (24in)*

14 Fake terracotta planter; *60cm (24in) × 65cm (26in)*

15 Fake carved stone bowl; *15cm (6in) × 35cm (14in)*

16 Fake terracotta tub; *50cm (20in) × 73cm (29in)*

container
principles

Choose healthy plants

Healthy and robust plants are the key to a successful container display. The plants need to look fantastic the moment they are planted up particularly when they are on display in a small courtyard area where they are will be subject to close scrutiny. Poor quality speciments will not only detract from the appearance of the plantings but will slow the growth of the display and prevent it from filling out the container.

In a busy garden centre the turnover of stock is quick enough for plants not to sit on the shelf long enough to deteriorate. Poorly maintained plants quickly show signs of neglect, overcrowding, poor nutrition and disease. To avoid these problems, always buy from a source where the plants look well tended and cared for. Plants that have been given space to grow rather than crowded together are likely to be in better health. Check the leaves for signs of pests and disease (*see page 146*) and do not be afraid to lift the plant out of its pot to inspect the health of its root system (*see opposite*). If there is a limited choice of plants available and the particular species you want for your display is of poor quality it can usually be revived by routine pruning and feeding but this will take time.

WATCHPOINTS

1   *Healthy roots are important. Avoid plants with poor or overcrowded root systems. Young plants that have very recently been potted up will not have an established root system and if they are lifted out, the potting compost will fall away. Look for plants that are sufficiently established to hold the potting compost together but where the roots are not a solid mass up against the pot edge. Pot-bound plants are slower to establish when planted into your container because water cannot easily penetrate the root ball.*

3   *Tip the plant out of its pot and look for signs of grubs or insects that might be eating the roots.*

4   *It is better to buy a small, healthy looking plant than a large, untidy one just because it has flowers. In the long term, the smaller one will grow and provide you with a better display.*

5   *Choose plants from the edge of a plant tray or display stand; these plants will have had access to more light and space to grow and should be more compact and sturdy.*

6   *Beware of trays of bedding plants where one or two plants are wilting. They may just be dry but they may also be suffering root disease which will spread to the other plants in your container. A gentle tug will help you determine if their roots are sound.*

In containers, plants are grown in close proximity to one another and have to compete for nutrients and water. Give each container planting the best chance of survival by carefully selecting only good quality, healthy plants.

Signs of poor health

General poor condition

Avoid plants that do not look healthy on first appearance. On closer inspection, moss and weeds growing on the surface of the potting compost indicate the plant has been in its pot for too long and is likely to be pot bound and undernourished. Spots and speckles on the leaves or pieces eaten away may indicate damage from pests and diseases.

PLANTS PARTICULARLY PRONE INCLUDE:

Alyogyne

Buxus

Hedera varieties

Helichrysum

Tibouchina

Pot-bound roots

Check the roots of the plant before you buy it by lifting it out of its plastic container. A pot-bound plant with its roots packed in a tight mesh will take longer to establish itself in a container display than a plant whose roots can be seen just spreading into the potting compost around the edge of the pot.

PLANTS PARTICULARLY PRONE INCLUDE:

Agave americana

Aegopodium podagraria.'Variegata'

Chlorophytum comosum

Heuchera

Lamium 'Hermann's Pride'

Leymus arenarius

Yellowing leaves

These are a sign that the plant is undernourished or has root problems because once the plant has used up all the nitrogen in its potting compost it will carry nitrogen away from the older leaves to the younger ones, causing the older ones to turn yellow. Nitrogen is a vital element for the production of chlorophyll, the pigment that traps light energy for the plant.

PLANTS PARTICULARLY PRONE INCLUDE:

Anthemis puncata subsp. *cupaniana.*

Asparagus densiflorus.

Cordyline australis

Lotus maculatus

Petasites japonicus

Leggy stems

Plants need good light levels to grow and if they do not have access to enough light then their stems will grow tall in an effort to reach the light source. This leads to straggly growth that is unable to physically support itself. The long stems are weak and are likely to break in windy weather. Very often these leggy stems also have softer growth and are prone to fungal attack.

PLANTS PARTICULARLY PRONE INCLUDE:

Argyranthemum varieties

Dahlia varieties

Kleinia seneciodes

Melianthus major

Pelargonium tomentosum

Prepare containers for planting

Before planting up a long-term container display, it is worth checking the pot over to make sure it is in good condition, particularly if it is going to stand outside all winter. Any cracks or chips in terracotta, ceramic or stone-based materials can be filled with an epoxy resin to prevent the crack from spreading futher and letting in water which may lead to frost damage (*see page 148*). Long cracks in terracotta can be held together by copper wire "stitching". The copper wire is threaded through holes drilled either side of the split or the split can be patched inside with fibreglass matting.

Container cleaning

For many people, including myself, one of the main attractions of choosing terracotta as a container material is the colour patina it develops with age. After several seasons outdoors, terracotta pots will accumulate layers of salts and algae on their surface. To prepare an old terracotta pot for planting, use a stiff brush and plenty of water and scrub it inside only. This will prevent any pest or disease from a previous occupant contaminating the new potting compost. Terrazzo containers can be scrubbed out with a kitchen scourer and water, while plastic pots can be prepared for planting with soapy water and a soft cloth to avoid any abrasive action which may damage the pot interior.

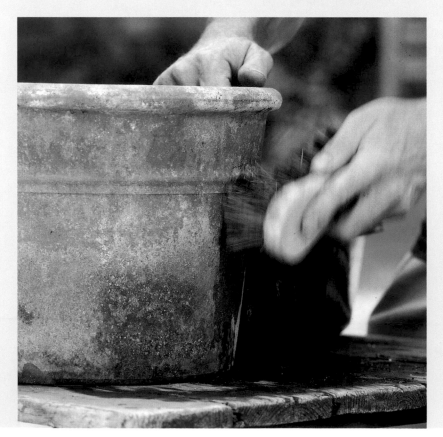

WORK SAFELY

If you are using a electric drill and an extension cable outdoors, do not let them get wet. Wear protective eye goggles during drilling and hammering to prevent sharp chips of stone or metal causing damage. The newly formed drainage hole will have also sharp, rough edges.

Container drainage

Drilling holes in ceramic

Good drainage is absolutely essential to grow plants successfully in containers. Some pots intended as plant containers have no drainage hole in the base or have only a small inadequate hole. To improve drainage, drill a large hole in their base. To do this:

◁ Turn the pot upside-down and using an electric drill and a masonry bit, drill a series of small holes in the base. Drill them as close together as is practical.

▷ Using a hammer carefully knock out the material between the holes to make one large single hole.

A small masonry drill bit is easier to use than a large diameter bit. It puts less stress on the material and can prevent large cracks from forming and so prevent the pot from breaking.

Drilling holes in metal

◁ Mark your holes using a centre punch or nail. Drill the hole using a large steel drill bit. Before you drill thin metals, place a block of wood under the metal surface to support it. For safety, hammer down sharp metal edges with a wooden dowel.

Placing crocks for drainage

▷ The purpose of crocks or stones is to ensure the free passage of water through the potting compost to the drainage hole. Arrange the crocks over the drainage hole so that you create as many cavities as possible. Larger curved pieces of broken terracotta pots are ideal for this.

Choose the right potting compost

The well-being of container-grown plants depends on the supply of light, nutrients and water. Both nutrients and water are obtained via the potting compost and different plants have different needs. The perfect growing conditions for each and every plant can be difficult to achieve in one pot where, for example, you might have drought-tolerant succulents next to thirsty leafy plants and yet it has always surprised me just how adaptable plants are. In my experience, as long as I use a free-draining compost that retains moisture well and has an "open" soil structure to allow oxygen to aerate the plant roots, then the plants will grow happily. The only plant species that will not grow in any type of potting compost are lime-hating plants such as Rhododendrons, Pieris, Calluna, and Restios.

Peat-based compost

This became the container gardening growing medium of choice for commercial growers and garden centres because of its ablity to retain water and air. It is also light and easy to transport. Its major drawback is that it contains no nutrients and all nutrients have to be added to the soil, making regular feeding or the use of controlled-release fertilisers essential. Also, peat-based potting composts can be difficult to rewet when they have dried out. Raw peat is naturally acidic which makes it ideal as the base for ericaceous compost.

Coir-based compost

Produced from coconut waste which is a renewable resource, coir-based compost was developed as an environmentally friendly alternative to peat. When first introduced, the properties of coir-based composts were not as impressive as other types but they now have improved water retention, soil hygiene and nutrition. Although nutrition and trace elements are present, liquid feed needs to be applied regularly to plants grown in this medium for best results.

They require a lime-free mix which is commonly known as ericaceous compost.

My preferred potting compost is loam-based and has about 20 per cent organic matter added in the form of peat or coir fibre to help retain water. To keep the potting compost "open" and fully aerated, try not to firm down the potting compost when planting up the display as this will drive air out and limit root growth.

Here, we describe the merits and drawbacks of the four main potting composts available to the container gardener to help you draw your own conclusions about which one is best suited to your planting needs.

Peat-free compost

As well as coir-based compost, there are several other peat-free alternatives available made from ingredients like cocoa shells, sawdust, straw, woodchips and bark. The last of these, bark, has been most studied and developed. It has established itself as an important and renewable ingredient in peat-free compost and is produced on a large-scale. It is usually partially broken down by composting to help dissipate any harmful plant toxins before being made into potting compost. Its natural nutrient level is not high so regular feeding of plants grown in bark is required.

Loam-based compost

This mix contains a high proportion of sterilised soil and is like buying good quality garden soil in a bag. Though there is a standard formula for loam- or soil-based composts, the quality varies. In most cases, extra organic matter is needed to improve the soil structure and water-holding capacity. Plants in loam-based composts do not need regular feeding: this compost contains nutrients and tiny particles called colloids which help retain any nutrients that already exist in the soil. This soil is heavy which can be useful to anchor exposed plantings.

Reduce the weight of containers

In most garden sites, the weight and scale of a container planting only becomes an issue when the pot has to be transported to a new location, or placed on a balcony or roof terrace above ground level which can only carry a limited load. Whenever possible, try to move your pot to its final position before you plant it up. The drainage material and potting compost increases the pot weight dramatically and then as soon as the potting compost has been watered it will become impossible to shift. Trying to move a heavy pot not only puts strain on your back but you also risk damaging a large container that was probably quite expensive. Thin-walled ceramic pots are likely to crack, metal can bend, and the base of a ceramic or resin pot may chip if rocked when full.

Halving pot weight

One way to keep down the overall weight of a large container planting is to use a lightweight potting compost. Loam-based potting composts are the heaviest so opt for a peat-, coir- or bark-based mix instead. Alternatively, you can reduce the total volume of potting compost used in the planting by only filling half the pot with soil and padding out the rest with a lightweight material. My technique involves a two-stage approach. First I place an empty upturned plastic pot inside the large container to fill the internal space and then I fill in around the plastic pot with drainage gravel. Only one third of the space is then left to fill with potting compost. When trying to reduce the weight of a container, bear in mind that for plantings intended to last for several years the more compost there is in a pot the healthier the plants will be. Any excessive reduction in potting compost volume may damage plant health.

Step 1

A large, round pot can be rolled along on its base rather than picked up. Take care when rolling terracotta and other ceramics on hard surfaces not to chip the base. Ask for help when lifting large pots or use a sack truck.

Step 2

Find a large plastic pot that fits upside-down inside your pot. It is likely to make a watertight seal when wedged into place so cut V-shaped notches in the rim with secateurs to allow for drainage.

Step 3

Make sure that there is at least 30-35cm (12-14in) from the rim down to plastic pot to allow for a suitable depth of potting compost for plant growth. A layer of gravel, or lightweight beads, will help keep the drainage holes clear of potting compost.

Step 4

Fill the container with potting compost. Peat-, coir- or bark-based composts are lighter than loam-based mixes.

Other weight reducers

Lightweight ceramic beads

This aggregate made from expanded balls of clay has an open, honeycomb-like structure and is both tough and lightweight. Ceramic beads are able to absorb water and so provide a small reserve of moisture and nutrients. Because of these beneficial properties a higher proportion of ceramic beads to potting compost can be used to fill a container to keep its weight down.

Moving containers

Container stands on wheels

Sooner or later you will need to move a large, full container either to change your display or to move you plants into a frost-free site over winter. One simple method is to use a low wooden platform on castors. Tip the pot back to slip the platform under the pot base. As long as you have a hard surface to run the pot along, these stands on wheels make moving very easy.

Polystyrene

Chunks of broken-up polystyrene will help bulk out the interior of a pot with virtually no weight gain. The best source of polystyrene are the trays that bedding plants are sold in at garden centres. Although you are creating a second use for this waste product, polystyrene is not biodegrable and will sit in the base of the pot forever so try to keep its use to a minimum.

Sack trucks

The professional sack truck is the easiest to use because its platform can be placed under a tilted pot with no lifting. An old blanket will protect the pot surface from scratches in transit. Alternatively, a low-cost solution is to slide a sheet of heavy-duty polythene under your pot and then drag the sheet along the ground bringing the pot with you This method does the least damage to a full and spreading planting.

Plant up for success

There are dozens of combinations and styles that can be achieved when planting up container displays. There are no set rules and I would encourage you to experiment with your own design ideas and not to let minor setbacks put you off. The following step-by-step method is intended to show you the basic skills in planting up a large traditional-style pot where one tall feature plant is surrounded by a mix of smaller flower and foliage plants. Knowing the different growth rates, heights and spreads of your plant selection helps to produce a well-proportioned display. With less familiar plants, however, this understanding only comes with experience as plants do not always behave as described on their label, and one may thrive in a container setting while another may fail.

Step 1

Work out your planting plan To establish a design, I think that it is easiest to work with the actual plants. Keep them in their plastic pots and arrange them on the surface of the potting compost so that you get a visual idea of how they will all fit together in the display. Once you are happy with the effect, arrange the plants in the same pattern on the ground and then one by one, lift them out of their pots and plant them up.

Step 2

Work from the middle of the display Establish your central feature plant and then work out from this point, planting up your tallest growers first and gradually moving down the scale to your shortest. Plant in a systematic way so that plants of the same type are evenly spaced across the pot surface.

Planting tips

1   *Water all plants well before adding them to the display. Soak in a bucket of water any that are particularly dry.*

2   *Keep the soil structure "open" and aerated and do not over-firm the potting compost around the plants.*

4   *Do not worry about creating symmetrical patterns as they will be blurred as the planting grows up.*

5   *Consider which side your planting design will be viewed from so you do not waste plants.*

6   *Put inexpensive bedding plants, such as Lobelia, amongst your main players to cover the compost before the larger plants develop. Though the bedding plants will be hidden when the planting matures, they offer a degree of interest during the early stages.*

7   *Arrange the longest trailing stems so that they face inwards rather than outwards – covering the potting compost will make the display look more established.*

Step 3

Positioning small plants Even though some plants are small, I always try to use them to best effect in an arrangement. To achieve this, I often tilt the plant on its side so that its best foliage or flowers face out towards the rim of the pot. Some of the root ball may be left exposed on the soil surface but as long as it is kept moist the plant will thrive.

Step 4

Filling out for a full effect Once you have finished planting up, add some more potting compost to fill the container to about 2.5cm (1in) below the rim. Take a look at your finished efforts to see, even at this early stage of plant growth, if the arrangement looks balanced. Reposition plants if you need to. When you are satisfied, water the display thoroughly.

Maintain plants regularly

A container planting should really be treated just like a garden but on a smaller scale. It requires the same amount of attention as your favourite flower border if you want it to look its best all year.

Each pot is only capable of holding a limited amount of soil and water to sustain the plants so the nutrients in the soil and water need topping up on a regular basis during the growing season to promote healthy leaf growth and flower production. As the season progresses, there are regular maintenance tasks to perform. The spent flowers will need deadheading, and trailing stems and vigorous plants in containers need trimming back so that they do not overwhelm the other plants in the display or the pot and ruin the balanced appearance of the display.

Soil compaction

Preventing soil compaction

The regular pounding effect of water on the potting compost surface creates a hard outer crust that prevents water and air from penetrating this top layer. Not surprisingly, loam-based potting composts (*see page 136*) are more prone to compaction than soil-free composts. Ways to avoid the problem involve dissipating the force of the water by watering onto another hard surface (*see below*), onto a stone or bark mulch, or sinking a small flower pot into the potting compost and watering into that.

Opening up the soil structure

Once the soil has become compacted it needs to be broken up. For large pot surfaces, use a hand fork or, for smaller pots, a kitchen fork or piece of stick. In mature plantings, the potting compost surface can also be bound up by roots. Use a hand fork to ease the roots apart and allow water to penetrate more easily. Alternatively, repot large plantings (*see page 152*), remove the top layer of roots and potting compost, and replace with new compost to free up the soil structure.

Deadheading

By preventing old flowers from setting seed, deadheading promotes the formation of new flowers. Picking off spent flowers also prevents them from falling back into the display and rotting which, in turn, rots the plant stems and foliage. This is a problem for Begonias and Pelargoniums and especially Regal Pelargoniums.

Some plants need to be deadheaded purely for cosmetic reasons. For example, I always remove the lower, spent flowers of Canna because they detract from the rest of the display. With Argyranthemum, I shear off all the flowers in one go to encourage a beautiful second flush of colour.

PLANTS THAT NEED DEADHEADING

Anthemis	*Osteospermum*
Begonia	*Pelargonium*
Canna	*Petunia*
Dahlias	*Solenostemon*
Nicotiana	*Verbena*

Feeding

Plants grown in the confines of a container have a restricted root run and therefore limited access to nutrients. In crowded containers, there is a higher than usual plant density and the supply of nutrients in the potting compost is quickly exhausted. Controlled-release fertiliser pellets mixed into the potting compost at planting time will provide a steady supply of food to your plants to sustain them. These fertilisers in pellet form are also available to buy as pellet clusters, designed to be pushed into the surface of the potting compost immediately after planting. A reliable way of providing instant nutrition is to water the plants with a soluble powder feed at fortnightly intervals (*see right*), thereby you can adjust the amount or frequency of feed and respond quickly to your plants' needs.

Cut back trailing stems

It is unlikely that all the plants within your display are of equal vigour so some management of the more vigorous is necessary if they are not to overwhelm the lesser plants. Climbers and scrambling plants whose very nature it is to climb over and smother their neighbours are usually the main culprits. Keep their growth in check by regular pinching out and pruning but always keep the overall shape and balance of the display in your sights when cutting back. This may mean only cutting out some of the unruly shoots and leaving a few climbing strands to make their way through your feature plant.

Trimming back foliage is all part of the ongoing maintenance of a planting and can be compared to the regular tasks you carry out in the garden by way of weeding flower beds, tying in, pruning and staking stems without which the garden looks out of control. Take time to stand back from your container and assess the overall planting design. Be prepared to cut out shoots that are growing in the wrong place or support lanky stems with canes if this improves its visual appeal.

Step 1: remove untidy growth

If you create the ideal conditions for your container-grown plants it can lead to exceptional growth which needs to be trained in the right direction or pruned back. This *Helichrysum petiolare* threatens to engulf the palm in the centre and because the effectiveness of the planting relies on a balance between the two, I am trimming it back and removing its yellow flowers, which I dislike.

Step 2: reshaping the display

The aim when reshaping a planting is to remove enough growth to restore a balance to the design but in such a way that it appears as if little has been altered. To achieve this, cut back stems to a side shoot or take out whole shoots completely. When cutting back thick shoots, cut the stem at a downward angle to hide the cut ends as these often turn white and look unattractive.

TRAILING PLANTS THAT MAY NEED CUTTING BACK

Bidens ferulifolia

Dichondra 'Silver Falls'

Geranium 'Anne Folkard'

Hedera varieties

Helichrysum petiolare

Kleinia senecioides

Lamium galeobdolon Hermann's Pride'

Lotus berthelotii

Lotus maculatus

Lysimachia nummularia 'Aurea'

Osteospermum jucundum

Pelargonium tomentosum

Petunia Trailing varieties

Plectranthus ciliatus

Plectranthus madagascariensis 'Variegated Mintleaf'

Plectranthus zatarhendii

Tropaeolum majus

Train pot-grown climbers

Rather than relying on one large central plant for height in your display, consider using climbing plants and, if the structural support is elegant, it can provide some interest before the climber becomes established.

There are a range of supports available including garden canes, plastic "sticks", metal spirals, wood or metal trellis, and also simple metal rods which can be used on their own or to create a wigwam structure. I prefer to use natural Hazel sticks cut from a coppiced tree in my own garden. In my opinion, their less than uniform shape adds to the charm of a planting. Their rough, natural surface is ideal for climbers of all types to cling to, be they twining plants such as *Thunbergia alata* or plants with grasping petioles or tendrils like *Rhodochiton atrosanguineus*. Ordinary shrub prunings can also be effective as natural canes if carefully selected.

When tying plants to smooth bamboo garden canes, first tie the garden string to the cane just above a node and wrap it around the node at least two times. This will prevent the fastening from slipping.

Avoid smooth canes

Metal rods and spirals make very stylish supports when trying to create a modern planting but they are not actually very useful as plant supports. Their metal surface is so smooth and shiny that they offer very little for the young plants to cling to and any attempt to tie plants to them with string usually ends with the whole lot just slipping down in a heap at the bottom of the poles!

Encouraging young stems

Most climbers will eventually start climbing the support you have given them but to speed the process, carefully tie on the stems of young plants to the canes. By first tying the string to the support and then tying a loose knot around the stem you avoid damaging tender young stems while allowing room for the stem to thicken as the plant matures.

CLIMBERS FOR GROWING IN CONTAINERS

Aconitum helmsleyanum

Clematis

Cobaea scandens

Eccremocarpus scaber

Hedera varieties

Ipomoea lobata and *I. tricolor*

Lapageria rosea

Lathyrus odoratus

Maurandya barclayana

Passiflora varieties

Plumbago auriculata

Rhodochiton atrosanguineus

Senecio macroglossus 'Variegata'

Sollya heterophylla

Thunbergia alata

Tropaeolum peregrinum and *T. tuberosum*

Tweedia caerulea

Combat common pests and diseases

If you were to take a look at the extensive list of pests and diseases that could affect your container plants you may well be discouraged from gardening altogether. In theory, within the confined space of a pot, a disease will quickly infect all the inhabitants but, in truth, if the plants are healthy to start with they will have the natural resources to fend off attack and few diseases will cause irreversible damage. Check your plantings daily for any signs of ill health and always take swift action. Where possible, I have chosen to feature plants (*see pages 26-115*) that are known for their reliablility when grown in containers and their resistance to pests and diseases. Any plant species that need special care to keep them in good health are noted in the Plant Directory (*see pages 154-185*).

Slugs and snails

Typical damage is irregular holes chewed in leaves, but if there is no sign of a slime trail suspect some other pest. Chemical deterrents usually contain Aluminium sulphate or Metaldehyde. Non-chemical means include slug traps baited with beer that the creatures fall into and drown. To protect individual pots, wrap a copper-based barrier tape around the pot. I also check my pots in the evening and pick off any slugs or snails that I see.

PLANTS PARTICULARLY AT RISK INCLUDE:

Hostas

Cannas

Dahlias

Eucomis

Impatiens

Ipomoeae batatas 'Blackie'

Viola

Aphids

These prolific creatures are the bane of gardeners and, encouraged by warm weather, they multiply rapidly. Depending upon the time of year there are both winged and flightless adults. They attack the soft growing tips of plants often causing distortion of leaves and the destruction of flower buds. Chemical aphid sprays are available at garden centres but for small infestations it is often more effective to pinch out the damaged tips.

PLANTS PARTICULARLY AT RISK INCLUDE:

Argyranthemum

Dahlia

Fatsia japonica

Helichrysum petiolare

Verbena

Viola

Vine weevil

This pest likes containers possibly because the sterilised potting compost used contains none of its natural enemies. The brown-headed, white C-shaped grubs feed on roots from late summer to late spring causing wilting and death. The adults are flightless beetles that chew unsightly but not fatal notches in leaf edges (*seen in picture on large leaf*). Watering in parasitic nematodes once the compost has warmed up helps limit damage.

PLANTS PARTICULARLY AT RISK INCLUDE:

Aeonium

Begonia

Echeveria

Euonymus 'Emerald 'n' Gold'

Heuchera

Pelargonium

Prevention

Trying to keep your plants free from pests and diseases is easier than trying to eradicate an established outbreak.

It is impossible to completely prevent pests and diseases establishing themselves on your plants but resistance can be encouraged by growing strong, robust plants free from the weakening effects of drought or poor nutrition that make them prone to attack.

Insect populations can build very quickly particularly in warm weather, so it is essential to make regular inspections and then act quickly to treat the first sign of disease or insect attack. Seek out the pests and remove them by spraying, rubbing or wiping off the culprits or simply prune out the affected part. Do not discard infected prunings on the compost heap. Burn them so that they do not have the opportunity to re-infect the planting.

In a large and full planting, infestations of insect pests can very go unnoticed until they are out of control. Check the growing tips and the undersides of the leaves regularly as they are the most likely places to harbour pests. Interstingly, hairy or scented leaves, such as those of Pelargonium 'Lady Plymouth' shown above, are usually less prone to insect attack.

WATCHPOINTS

1   *Insects seek shelter on the undersurface of the leaf and are often concentrated around the main leaf veins where food is plentiful. Examine the plants carefully because many insects are well-camouflaged —green caterpillars are easy to miss and aphids can tuck themselves into the young, rolled-up leaves of plants like Canna. Rub or wipe off the insects and eggs.*

2   *Wet foliage encourages the spread of fungal diseases so take care when watering. This is particularly true of dense fleshy foliage such as Begonias.*

3   *Spent flowers lying on top of foliage encourages rot. Regular dead-heading or picking over will help to avoid rot as well as keeping the display looking tidy.*

4   *Be aware that overfeeding container plantings with high nitrogen feeds can promote growth that is soft and prone to disease, creating an easy target for sap-sucking insects.*

5   *Act quickly! Scientific estimates suggest that in one season when conditions are ideal, a single aphid can give rise to several thousand tons of aphids if all its offspring survive.*

6   *Potting composts are available with in-built systemic insecticides. These are then taken up by the plants giving them long-term protection against a wide range of pests and diseases. Do not use systemic insecticides if you are growing culinary herbs or food crops.*

Protect pots and plant roots

The main enemy of container plantings and modern clay pots, in particular, is freezing weather conditions. We cannot control the weather but we can limit its damaging effects on plants and vulnerable pots, especially during the winter months by taking preventative measures.

The damage caused to pots is the result of wet potting compost inside the terracotta container freezing. As the water freezes it expands, pushing upwards. If the pot has a narrow neck, it is likely to crack and then break apart under the pressure. Lining pots with air-filled wrapping material will act as a buffer when the compost expands. Storing clay pots indoors when not in use is also a good idea. This action will prevent damp seeping into cracks, freezing and causing the pot surface to flake away.

Signs of frost damage

The quality and thickness of a terracotta pot will determine how resistant it is to frost damage. Machine-made pots are more prone to splitting and shaling than hand-thrown pots where the container has been worked into shape out of a single block of clay. Still in use today are some one-hundred-year-old clay pots that have been left outside every winter – testament to the durability of quality handmade containers.

Lining pots

When the potting compost expands and sets solid in freezing weather, pots at risk from frost damage can be lined with plastic air-filled sheets. This protective lining works because each air-bubble gets squashed against the pot interior to absorb the expansion and then it re-forms as the air temperature rises and the compost softens. With large valuable pots, I use large air-filled plastic envelopes originally used for packing fragile items for transport, placed in the middle of the potting compost.

Protect tender plants

Many fast-growing tender perennials are inexpensive to buy so the cost of over-wintering them in a heated glasshouse, particularly in cold areas, cannot be justified. It makes better financial sense to buy new stock each year. However, large specimens or more unusual plants are harder to replace and are worth bringing in under glass to protect them from extreme cold and frost.

Other tender plants such as Melianthus, Canna, and Dahlias can be cut down, dug up and stored as dormant plants in a well-ventilated garage or shed. In this state, they need no light but should be kept cool, frost-free, and just moist through the winter.

All tender plants should be kept dry in cold temperatures to prevent their roots rotting and to concentrate the sap to form a natural "antifreeze".

Wrapping tender plants in fleece

If greenhouse or conservatory space is limited, borderline hardy can be left outside as long as they are given protection during particularly cold spells. Use straw, layers of sacking or plastic bubble-wrap as insulation. Wrap this around the pot and the plant but be aware this is not a permanent solution. To shelter tall foliage plants such as Cordyline and Phormium against the effects of cold winds, wrap up the plants in several layers of horticultural fleece – again, this is only for emergency use.

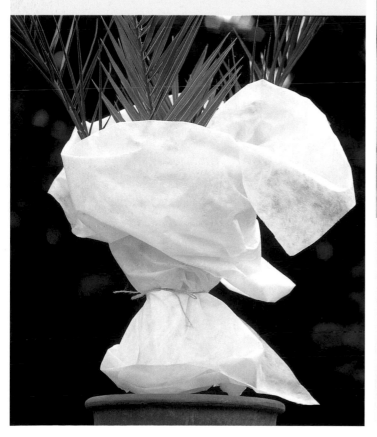

Moving tender plants indoors

Tender evergreen plants can be lifted out of their containers, potted up, and brought into the shelter of a glasshouse or conservatory before the first frosts. Plants like Aeonium, Agave, Cordyline, Plectranthus, Solenostemon, Abutilon, Aspidistra, Kalanchoe and Echeveria make dramatic indoor specimens before being moved back outside the next summer. If space is short, take cuttings in late summer and over-winter smaller plants; they will quickly put on growth the following spring.

Keep potting compost moist

Growing plants in containers is a creative and fun form of gardening but it has one major drawback; the plants have to be watered and, in summer, this can mean twice a day. With just one or two pots that sit outside the back door, this is an easy job, but if the containers are arranged over a large garden or you have a huge number of them, then watering becomes a major chore. Running out the length of hose or walking back and forth to the garden tap with a watering can be very time-consuming. There are ways to make this job easier and quicker as outlined below.

A good tip to remember when watering pots is to always water from the back and try not to water in the same spot each time as this can create a hole in the plant material that spoils the effect.

Automatic watering

Auto-irrigation systems

This involves setting up a simple irrigation system whereby each pot is fed by one or more capillary tubes from an outside water supply. Care is needed in regulating flow so as not to flood or deprive your pots. It can be operated manually or by an automatic timing device that irrigates the pots at pre-set times. This system does not take into account the moisture in the soil but more sophisticated systems will. In hard water areas, check that the nozzles do not become blocked.

Capilliary method

This low-tech method will water pots while the water supply in the receptacle lasts. Simply place a full bucket of water or a watering-can above the level of your pot. Attach one end of a strip of wet greenhouse capillary matting to your vessel of water and attach the other end to the potting compost. Water will flow out of the vessel down to your pot until the vessel is empty. Some experimentation may be needed to establish the right thickness of strip to create a steady drip rate.

Retaining moisture

Mulches

A decorative covering of pebbles, stone chips or glass not only looks attractive but keeps the potting compost moist and preserves water by reducing evaporation from the soil surface. This is useful when growing large single specimens, such as Japanese acers that enjoy cool, moist roots. Mulches also prevent dirty soil splashes on the pot and plant during watering.

Water-retaining crystals

These can be added to the soil to provide a reserve of moisture for the roots should the soil become dry, and for this reason they are useful in hanging baskets which tend to dry out quickly. Mix the potting compost and dry crystals together then water thoroughly. Take care not to add too many as the expanding crystals will push themselves and the soil out of the pot.

Environmental issues

Water is a precious resource and, with many supplies being metered, a costly commodity. For this reason, as much use should be made of collected rainwater as possible. Rainwater is also essential for irrigating lime-hating plants in hard-water areas. Careful watering of each individual containers with a watering-can or hose is also far more economical than using a sprinkler.

Set up your auto-irrigation system carefully to maximise water use and avoid undue run off. In many regions to comply with local authority legislation you must fit a non-return valve between your water supply and any irrigation system you install. This is intended to protect household water supplies from being contaminated if dirty water is siphoned back into the mains.

Know when to repot

Plants grown in pots over a long period of time will produce an expansive root system that exhaust the potting compost of nutrients. The roots also make it difficult for oxygen to penetrate the soil as they tend to choke up every pore of the soil.

Regular repotting supplies fresh nutrients, opens up the soil structure, and so promotes new root growth. The signs that indicate when a plant is in desperate need of re-potting include:

- Poor growth and yellowed leaves.
- The plant wilts more quickly than well-potted specimens and needs constant watering.
- The surface of the potting compost is matted with a web of roots.
- When lifted out of the pot, root-bound plants reveal a solid mass of roots pressed against the pot.

Step 1

Large plants in big pots can be extremely heavy and often reluctant to come out of their pots. Tip the pot on its side so that you do not have to lift the weight of the compost and to get a better grip on the plant. A stubborn plant might need two people, one to hold the pot the other to pull out the plant. If the plant is stuck, give it a thorough watering to help release the roots' grip on the side of the pot, or run a long-bladed knife around the inside of the pot to free up the root ball.

Step 2

Once the rootball is free tease out the roots from the potting compost and shake off most of the old soil. Loosen the root ball by rubbing the roots through your fingertips to separate out the matted strands. Use a strong jet of water from a hose to wash out the soil stuck between the roots.

WATCHPOINTS

1 When potting up plants for long-term displays, use a pot with a smooth interior to make removal of the plant at a later date straightforward.

2 Avoid using pots where the neck of the pot is a smaller than the body of the pot. The plant will be impossible to remove without breaking the pot apart.

3 Planting the display inside a pot liner is a good idea for large specimens like large clipped topiary. This way the pot exterior is just an outer jacket and the plant can be pulled out in its liner through a side panel that comes off. This is much less effort than having to lift an established plant out of a container.

Step 3

Up to one third of the roots can be cut off Cut through a few of the thicker roots and remove whole sections. Keep the finer roots intact as these are useful to help re-establish the plant. The dirt and grit around the roots will damage your secateur blades so use an old or cheap pair.

Step 4

Replace the drainage material in the pot base and put a layer of potting compost on top. Position the pared-down root ball and fill in around it with fresh, dry compost. Push compost around the root ball and then shake the plant and pot to make sure that compost settles in any gaps. Do not firm down the compost. Water thoroughly and keep the planting out of hot sunshine and drying winds for several weeks while the roots re-establish themselves.

container
plant directory

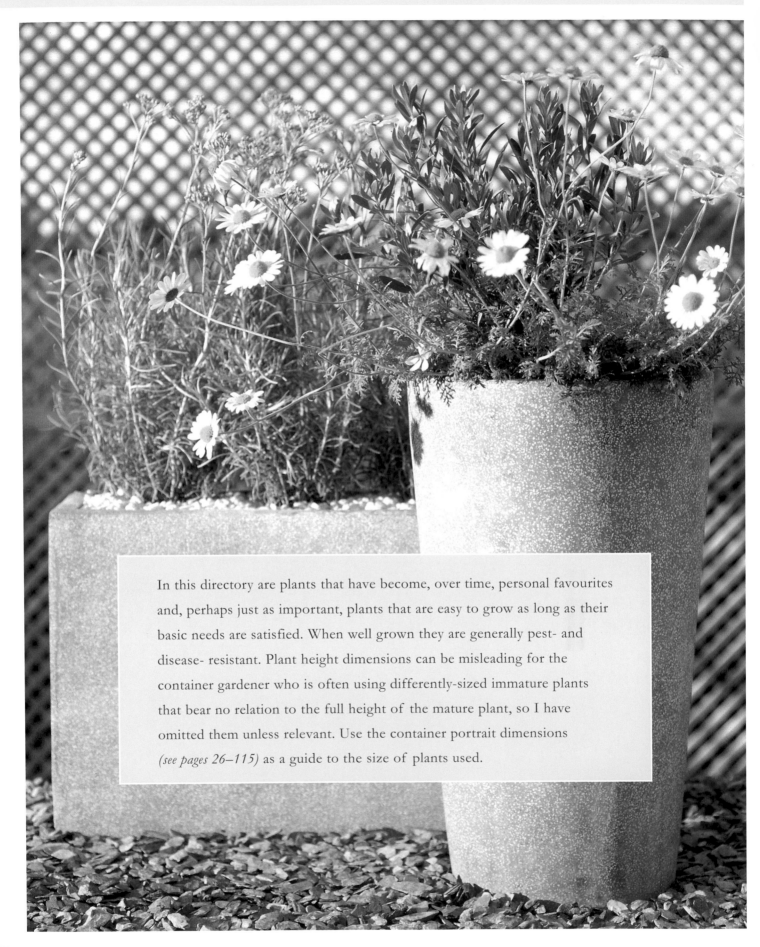

In this directory are plants that have become, over time, personal favourites and, perhaps just as important, plants that are easy to grow as long as their basic needs are satisfied. When well grown they are generally pest- and disease- resistant. Plant height dimensions can be misleading for the container gardener who is often using differently-sized immature plants that bear no relation to the full height of the mature plant, so I have omitted them unless relevant. Use the container portrait dimensions *(see pages 26–115)* as a guide to the size of plants used.

A

Abutilon 'Kentish Belle'

An open and arching shrub with considerable grace. The foliage is sparse making the flowers easily seen. They show up well against their dark wiry stems. **Cultivation** It needs canes to support its lax stems to give height if used as a container centrepiece. Sun/light shade. **Hardiness** Tolerates a few degrees of frost but is best kept above freezing during the winter.

See page 70

Abutilon 'Nabob'

An erect evergreen shrub with large maple-like leaves and heavy, sombre-looking, nodding flowers. Ideally suited as a centre plant in a display. **Cultivation** It is potentially a large shrub but it tolerates pruning and can be kept to a manageable size. Late summer cuttings produce vigorous plants for use the following summer. Sun. **Hardiness** Stands occasional winter temperatures as low as 0°C (32°F). A temperature of 10°C (50°F) will keep it flowering throughout the year.

See page 44

Adiantum capillus-veneris

A useful fern for providing soft texture amongst harder and shinier plants. Its wiry black stems are a feature that should be exploited. **Cultivation** Keep out of full sun and drying winds. Shearing off the foliage in spring will promote a sprouting of fresh new fronds. **Hardiness** Tolerates some cold but loses its leaves below freezing and is best kept at 5°C (41°F) or above.

See page 48

Aegopodium podagraria 'Variegatum'

This herbaceous perennial is an ornamental variety of an invasive weed. It is only slightly less vigorous than its weedy counterpart and a pot is the safest place for it. It is valuable for its good, clean cream-white variegation. **Cultivation** In spring, it bears fluffy white flowers. Cut them off to prevent them from seeding and detracting from the foliage. Sun or shade. **Hardiness** Fully hardy.

See page 102

Aeonium arboreum

A tender succulent with thick branching woody stems that bear fleshy terminal rosettes. **Cultivation** An easily cared for plant whose rosettes root easily if they are cut off just below the leaves and pushed into a gritty potting compost that is kept just moist. Sun or light shade. **Hardiness** Give a winter minimum of 8-10°C (46-50°F).

See page 76

Aeonium 'Zwartkop'

This is one of the most dramatic plants available for small-scale container gardening. **Cultivation** Tolerant of a wide range of conditions, growing well in the same pot alongside such unlikely companions as *Begonia rex*. Give it plenty of light. Be brave and cut back leggy plants. They will shoot from below the cut. In hardwater areas, keep water splashes off the foliage. **Hardiness** Give a winter minimum of 8-10°C (46-50°F).

See page 32

Agastache 'Apricot Sprite'

The subtle mix of colours provided by the stems, buds, flowers and foliage make this a plant of great value for restrained colour schemes. **Cultivation** Keep potting compost on the dry side to get the most intense colour from the grey-green foliage.Sun. **Hardiness** In well-drained potting compost this has stood several degrees of frost in my garden but, for guaranteed survival, offer frost protection, otherwise treat it as an annual.

See page 28

Agave americana 'Variegata'

A dramatic plant for the container gardener. It makes a robust rosette of thick, fleshy leaves armed with spines along their edges. **Cultivation** Can reach 2m (6ft) or more in height but its growth is slowed in a pot and it can be kept small for several years. Give it plenty of sun and good drainage. **Hardiness** Withstands the occasional frost but is happier with a winter minimum of between 5° and 8°C (41-46°F).

See page 76

Anthemis punctata subsp. *cupaniana*

This is an evergreen perennial plant valued for its silvery filigree foliage and freely produced flowers. It has a vigorous spreading habit, ideal for spilling out of pots. **Cultivation** Tidy up the plant by shearing off the first flush of flowers when they are over. More flowers will be produced. Sun. **Hardiness** Though quite hardy it dislikes wet and cold so provide exceptionally good drainage to help it through the winter.

See page 58

Antirrhinum (Luminaire Series)™ 'Trailing White'

White is eye-catching and can be a distraction but this Antirrhinum presents its colour in a way that blends into a planting. Its trailing habit and soft foliage make it a favourite. Regular dead-heading helps promote a continuous show of flowers. **Cultivation** Treat as a half-hardy annual and sow in gentle heat in late winter or early spring. Sun, light shade. **Hardiness** It flowers up to the first hard frost.

See page 54

Antirrhinum (Luminaire Series)™ 'Deep Trailing Yellow'

The flowers of this trailing snapdragon have a charm and light-heartedness that lifts and refreshes a planting. Flowers come in flushes but there are always flowers on the plant and they are produced over a long season. **Cultivation** and **Hardiness** Treat it the same as Antirrhinum 'Trailing White'. Sun, light shade.

See page 70

Alocasia sanderiana

A tender evergreen with striking leaves that add a touch of the tropical to a display. In ideal conditions the leaves grow to 30-40cm long but outdoors in a container they are often much smaller. **Cultivation** It needs warm summers and sheltered conditions to succeed outdoors. Keep it out of direct sun and drying winds. **Hardiness** A minimum of 15°C (59°F) is required to see this Alocasia safely through the winter.

See page 114

Aloe ferox

This is an all-over prickly succulent with loads of character. Mature plants reach 2m (6ft) in height but young plants make ideal architectural specimens for planting in a pot on their own. **Cultivation** Give it plenty of light especially in winter. Sun. **Hardiness** It needs a winter temperature of around 10°C (50°F) and keep the potting compost fairly dry.

See page 76

Alyogyne huegelii

The straggly, open habit and sparse foliage of this evergreen shrub have little to commend them but the flowers are of outstanding beauty. The silky blue petals unfurl into large saucer-like flowers. Set it amongst plants whose foliage is stronger and enjoy the flowers. **Cultivation** Pinching out shoot tips at the start of the season will encourage bushiness and greater numbers of flowers. Sun. **Hardiness** Protect from frost.

See page 62

Argyranthemum foeniculaceum

A shrubby plant ideal for a frothy summer effect. The grey-green foliage is finely cut and the long-stalked flowers are produced non-stop throughout the summer. **Cultivation** Late summer cuttings root easily and can be over-wintered as small plants that grow away quickly in spring. Pinch out growing tips to encourage bushiness. Benefits from regular deadheading. Sun. **Hardiness** Withstands the first few frosts but needs winter protection.

See page 110

Askiodiosperma paniculatum

This belongs to the *Restionaceae* family whose members are commonly known as Restios. This is a dwarf species that only grows to around 60cm (24in). It makes a very good architectural container specimen. **Cultivation** Must have lime-free potting compost and be watered with soft water – rainwater is ideal. Sun. **Hardiness** It will withstand moderate frost but in a container it is better kept frost-free during winter.

See page 92

Asparagus densiflorus

Many common houseplants make good container plants. This is one of them. It is perfect for filling in around the base of a planting to cover the bare potting compost when the planting is young. **Cultivation** An easily cared for plant but avoid dry conditions and scorching sun. Shade. **Hardiness** Treat it as a houseplant during the winter and plant out when the danger of frost has past.

See page 64, 98

Aspidistra elatior

Despite being an old fashioned and much-derided plant, the Aspidistra is a very useful foliage plant whose long and broad leaves can be used as major structural elements in a planting. **Cultivation** Keep moist and out of direct sunlight and strong drying winds. Shade. **Hardiness** Although usually grown as a houseplant, *Aspidistra elatior* is tougher than you might imagine and tolerates several degrees of frost.

See page 64

Athyrium filix-femina 'Frizelliae'

This is an unusual deciduous fern with lobed leaflets that create all sorts of zigzag patterns and ruffs along their arching stems. It has a neatness and charm that never fails to draw attention. As with all ferns there is great beauty in the unfurling fronds in spring. **Cultivation** Providing it is kept moist this fern tolerates both shade and full sun. **Hardiness** Fully hardy.

See page 90

Athyrium niponicum var. pictum

This is one of my top-ten plants. The foliage has the most subtle combinations of colours with silvery grey, pink-purple and green blended together so delicately. Leaf colour varies so select a good form when you are buying. **Cultivation** It grows better in a neutral to acid potting compost. Keep moist and out of hot sunshine. Shade. **Hardiness** This is a hardy fern.

See page 90

Begonia 'Comtesse de Montesquieu'

Begonias with large and ornamental foliage, (usually hybrids of *Begonia rex*) are much underused as container plants. The range of colours is wide and both leaves and stems often have a hairy or dimpled texture. **Cultivation** Do not plant out until all danger of frost has past and the night time air temperature is up to 9-10°C (48-50°F). Prevent water getting into the crown. Shade. **Hardiness** A minimum temperature of 10°C (50°F) is required.

See page 106

Begonia 'Fire Flush'

The remarkably coloured leaves of 'Fire Flush' are held on stems covered in intensely red, dense hairs. Pale pink flowers are produced late in the season but do little to improve the appearance of the plant and are best removed. **Cultivation** and **Hardiness** as for *B.* 'Comtesse de Montesquieu'.

See page 106

Begonia 'Fireworks'

Fireworks' is one of the most dramatically coloured, foliage begonias. Its multicoloured leaves make it an ideal specimen for use on its own, but it also works well with a wide range of colours including pinks, whites, silver and primrose yellow.

Cultivation and **Hardiness** as for B.'Comtesse de Montesquieu'.

See page 94

B

Bacopa 'White Suttis 98'

This is a plant with tiny flowers and foliage but with a big impact. It grows in dense mats that spill out of pots and it flowers from spring until the first frosts. Other Bacopa varieties include pink and lavender-coloured forms and a variegated variety. **Cultivation** Easily grown and recovers well from the occasional drying out. **Hardiness** Treat as a tender annual.

See page 52

Begonia 'Connie Boswell'

A tall variety with long leaf stems and open growth. **Hardiness** and **Cultivation** as for *B.* 'Comtesse de Montesquieu'.

See page 94

Begonia 'Martin Johnson'

Another Begonia with outstanding foliage. The deeply cut leaves with jagged margins give it added drama. **Cultivation** and **Hardiness** as for *B.* 'Comtesse de Montesquieu'.

See page 94

Begonia 'Peace'

Given good growing conditions the leaves on this Begonia grow very large. Try it against finer foliage such as the filigree leaves of *Athyrium niponicum* var *pictum*. **Cultivation** and **Hardiness** as for *B.* 'Comtesse de Montesquieu'.

See page 94

Begonia 'Solid Silver'

A remarkable plant with very large, puckered leaves speckled and burnished with silver. **Cultivation** and **Hardiness** as for *B.* 'Comtesse de Montesquieu'.

See page 94

C

Begonia fuchsioides

This is a most un-begonia like Begonia. The upright stems bear small, toothed and glossy leaves and the vaguely fuchsia-like flowers hang in pendulous bunches. It is a vigorous plant and small plants can make 40-50cm (16-20in) in a season so young plants tucked in the base of a planting will become more prominent as the season progresses. **Cultivation** An easily grown plant that benefits from well-fed potting compost. **Hardiness** Frost tender.

See page 100

Bidens ferulifolia 'Golden Star'

Golden Star is a more compact version, though still vigorous, of the more wayward *B. ferulifolia* and is better suited to smaller arrangements. **Cultivation** Be prepared to cut it back should it overwhelm its neighbours. It will soon re-grow. Sun. **Hardiness** This is a tender perennial so either overwinter cuttings or buy in new plants in spring.

See page 70

Canna Orange Flower

There are many Canna hybrids available but they are often labelled incorrectly. If you can see the flower colour before you buy so much the better. Otherwise buy from a nursery with a reputation to uphold. **Cultivation** Easy, fast-growing plants. Sun. **Hardiness** Protect from frost. If space is limited the rootstock can be stored in a dark and cool but frost-free place over winter. Keep them just moist and protect from mice.

See page 100

Canna 'Pretoria'

This is also offered for sale as 'Striata' *C. malawiensis* 'Variegata' and 'Kapit'. It is a startling plant with its yellow striped leaves but it is made all the more amazing when it opens its large orange flowers. Unbeatable for tropical, flamboyant effect. **Cultivation** Feed and water it well to realise its full splendour. Sun. **Hardiness** Must be stored in a frost-free place overwinter.

See page 80

Canna musifolia

As a large foliage plant there is little to beat this Canna. It grows very tall and needs a large pot. It is shy to flower in Great Britain. **Cultivation** Keep well watered and feed regularly. Avoid planting it areas where the leaves can be damaged by windy weather. **Hardiness** It does not stand freezing but can be cut back and stored in a dormant state around 5°C (41°F).

See page 100

Calopsis paniculata

A wonderful South American Restio. The old foliage is lax and floppy while the new is upright giving the plant a permanently untidy look. It eventually makes a plant 2m (6ft) high but is worth keeping in a pot as long as possible and enjoying its feathery foliage at close quarters. **Cultivation** Needs acid conditions. Sun. **Hardiness** Tolerates short-term cold but is best kept above freezing.

See page 92

Canna 'Black Knight'

Broad dark leaves and intense red flowers make this an ideal centrepiece for a dramatic planting. **Cultivation** Give it plenty of water and feed regularly. Removing spent flowers keeps each flower spike looking its best. Take care when watering in hard water areas as deposits left by water splashes mark the leaves. **Hardiness** Does not tolerate freezing temperatures but can be cut back and stored in a dormant state around 5°C (41°F).

See page 88

Canna 'Durban'

Its combination of purple leaves, pink stripes and orange flowers must make this one the most garish of the Cannas but there is nothing better if you want a plant guaranteed to grab the attention. **Cultivation** Water well and feed regularly. Site it in plenty of light but out of the wind. Sun. **Hardiness** It does not stand freezing but can be cut back and stored in a dormant state around 5°C (41°F).

See page 40

Carex oshimensis 'Evergold'

A reliable and cheery stalwart for winter plantings. Its tufts of variegated, evergreen foliage go well with purple-leaved Heucheras and soft yellow winter pansies. Use it to brighten shady corners during the winter months. **Cultivation** It dislikes dry potting compost so water regularly. **Hardiness** Fully hardy.

See page 68

Carex comans 'Frosted Curls'

Nondescript green flowerheads borne on exceptionally long and graceful stems drape from a silvery green mound of tough narrow foliage. It becomes a very animated plant in windy weather. **Cultivation** An easily grown plant given a moist soil and a sunny site. Occasionally comb out dead leaves with your fingers. Sun. **Hardiness** Fully hardy and reliable for year-round effect.

See page 84

Carex phyllocephala "Sparkler"

Unlike most Carex, the leaves are arranged in whorls around an erect stem. It is most effective when grown in a low container where the leaves can be looked down on. **Cultivation** Keep watered and feed well. **Hardiness** My potted plants succumb to winter cold when left out in the open. Tucked up against a wall or given frost protection, they survive.

See page 68

Carex buchananii

There are several, very similar brown or "dead" grasses and all are useful for winter and summer effect. *C. buchananii* makes a robust upright tuft of evergreen leaves that have delightful curls at their leaf tips. **Cultivation** Dislikes waterlogged potting compost so ensure good drainage to see it through the winter. Sun. **Hardiness** With good drainage, it will survive several degrees of frost.

See page 82, 84

Carex flagellifera 'Coca-cola'

Another "dead" grass with evergreen tufted leaves and long-stalked brown flowerheads. Marvellous for hanging over the edge of a pot where the long flower stalks can trail down. **Cultivation** Does not like it too dry. Sun/light shade. **Hardiness** May be damaged by long-term cold weather below -10°C (14°F) but can generally be considered hardy.

See page 86, 108, 112

Carex morrowii 'Fisher's Form'

The leaves of this hardy evergreen are stiff and shiny with cream stripes on a dark green background and provide valuable, year-round foliage for a shady site. **Cultivation** Water regularly as it does not enjoy being dried out. Shade. **Hardiness** Though it stands several degrees of frost, it will benefit from the protection of a sheltered site.

See page 64

Chondropetalum mucronatum

This is a very architectural plant with the potential to grow to 1.5m (5ft) or more. The reed-like growth and unbranching structure gives the plant a primitive character. **Cultivation** Requires a well-drained but moisture-retentive acidic potting compost. Irrigate with soft water. Full sun. **Hardiness** Tolerates several degrees of frost but may be damaged by long-term cold.

See page 92

Convolvulus cneorum

A well-behaved shrubby Convolvulus with silver, evergreen leaves and white flowers that are produced over a long period from late spring to autumn. **Cultivation** Enjoys full sun and free-draining potting compost. The drier and sunnier the situation the more intense the leaf colour. Sun. **Hardiness** Tolerates a few degrees of frost but is likely to be damaged by persistent cold below - 6 or -7°C (23-21°F).

See page 42, 58, 84

Cordyline australis

Mature plants can be several metres tall but plants between 30cm (12in) and 1m (3ft) high are suitable for container gardening. Its bold fountain-like shape makes it the ideal centrepiece for large displays. Several varieties are available, some with multi-colour, striped leaves. **Cultivation** Give it full sun or light shade and a moist potting compost. **Hardiness** Tolerant of the occasional frost but likely to be damaged by persistent temperatures below freezing.

See page 36, 48

Cerinthe major 'Purpurascens'

A sophisticated-looking and fast-growing plant with flowers that unfurl from a spiral of buds. Flower and foliage colours are a perfect blend of blue-grey and purple. **Cultivation** An easy plant given good potting compost and plenty of light. Produces an abundance of easily germinated seed. Full sun. **Hardiness** Treat it as a half-hardy annual. Sow indoors in cool conditions and plant out when the danger of frost has passed.

See page 78

Ceropegia linearis subsp woodii

Use its hanging stems down the outside of tall pots to emphasise the vertical line. **Cultivation** A tolerant, easily grown plant that grows quickly once established. Sun or light shade. **Hardiness** Can be left out until the first frost after which it needs to be brought in for winter at a temperature between 8-10°C (46-50°F).

See page 110

Chlorophytum comosum 'Variegatum'

This is the Spider plant, a common houseplant but also a useful and underused foliage plant for container gardening. **Cultivation** Grow in a sheltered place to avoid the leaves being bent over by the wind. Easily propagated from the small "plantlets" that form on the end of arching shoots. Tolerates some dryness due to its water-storing tuberous roots but keep out of scorching sun. Shade. **Hardiness** Frost tender.

See page 36

Cordyline australis 'Torbay Red'

A striking plant for giving height and shape to the middle of a planting. Its red-purple colour offers plenty of scope for different colour combinations. **Cultivation** Give it full sun or light shade and a moist potting compost. **Hardiness** Tolerant of the occasional frost but likely to be damaged by persistent temperatures below freezing.

See page 66

Cordyline australis Purpurea Group

This name covers a range of plants with purple leaves of different shades. Shop around and select the deepest colour available. **Cultivation** Give it full sun or light shade and moist potting compost. **Hardiness** Tolerant of the occasional frost but likely to be damaged by persistent temperatures below freezing.

See page 28, 80

Crocosmia 'Star of the East'

Crocosmias are valuable for their foliage as well as their bright flowers. They come in colours from pale yellow to fiery red and in heights ranging from 40cm (16in) to over 1m (3ft). All are good plants for late summer colour. **Cultivation** Dormant corms can be planted in autumn amongst a hardy planting, or use young divisions in spring amongst tender plants. Full sun and moist potting compost. Sun. **Hardiness** Hardy.

See page 100, 108

Cuphea 'Tiny Mice'

Flowers of an intense colour with vaguely "mice-like" faces give this shrubby plant plenty of character. Its bushy habit and dark green leaves make it a good filler for the base of a display. **Cultivation** An easily-grown plant for full sun. Pinch out the shoot tips to encourage bushy growth. Sun. **Hardiness** A tender perennial that can be over-wintered at around 10°C (50°F).

See page 80

Cuphea hyssopifolia 'Alba'

Tiny white flowers and small leaves give this bushy little plant a busy, frothy look. Ideal for filling in around taller plants and for giving newly planted displays a fuller look. Pink and purple varieties are available. **Cultivation** An easy, trouble-free plant requiring no special conditions. Sun or shade. **Hardiness** A frost-tender perennial that needs a minimum winter temperature of at least 7°C (45°F).

See page 36

Cuphea ignea

A bushy evergreen shrub producing its tubular orange flowers in good numbers and over a long period. It provides interesting detail within a planting and is a good filler around more upright plants. **Cultivation** Pinch out shoot tips when young to encourage bushy growth. Easily propagated from seed or by cuttings taken in late summer. Sun. **Hardiness** Requires a minimum winter temperature of around 6°C (43°F).

See page 108

Dahlia 'Ragged Robin'

A recent introduction. Deeply cut, almost feathery foliage and small flowers with uneven petals give it a romantic and natural quality that is absent in the traditional large-flowered Dahlias. **Cultivation** Water well and feed regularly. Full sun or light shade. **Hardiness** Frost tender. Wait until the foliage is blackened by the frost then cut back the stems. Lift and store the tubers in a frost-free environment away from hungry mice.

See page 88

Dahlia 'Roxy'

Many Dahlias are too tall to be useful container plants but this short variety – with magenta flowers and almost black leaves – only grows to about 40cm (16in). **Cultivation** Water well and feed regularly. Full sun or light shade. **Hardiness** Frost tender. Wait until the foliage is blackened by the frost before cutting back the stems. Lift and store the tubers in a frost-free environment away from hungry mice.

See page 30

Dichondra 'Silver Falls'

A very good plant for providing dense trailing foliage. **Cultivation** Easily grown. Stems root readily if tucked into the potting compost giving rise to more shoots and even denser growth. It is slow to start but once established and the temperature warms up, it makes vigorous growth. Full sun. **Hardiness** A tender perennial that is likely to survive the first few frosts, but needs bringing in to a minimum winter temperature of 7°C (45°F).

See page 72, 74

Cussonia paniculata

Mature plants reach 4-5m (12-15ft) but younger specimens are ideal for architectural container displays. Few plants come near it for impressive foliage. **Cultivation** Ensure good drainage. Tolerant of occasional drying out. Sun. **Hardiness** Tolerates occasional frost but for guaranteed health keep at a minimum of 7°C (45°F) during the winter.

See page 72

D

Dahlia 'Bednall Beauty'

Its wonderful combination of glossy dark divided foliage and crimson flowers makes this worthy of a pot on its own. At around 50cm (20in) tall it is one of the shorter dahlias. **Cultivation** Water well and feed regularly. Full sun or light shade. **Hardiness** Frost tender. Wait until the foliage is blackened by the frost then cut back the stems. Lift and store the tubers in a frost-free environment away from hungry mice.

See page 112

E

Echeveria glauca

An important foliage plant. Try it in colour combinations with white, black, pink and purple. The multi-coloured flowers are fun but if they upset your colour scheme, cut them off. **Cultivation** An easy succulent that given moist potting compost will grow into large rosettes by the end of the season. Sun and light shade. **Hardiness** Frost tender. Over-winter at a minimum of 7°C (45°F).

See page 56

Elymus magellanicus

A well-behaved, clump-forming perennial grass with pale blue leaves. It can look scruffy so tidy up any dead leaves before planting and then periodically during the season. **Cultivation** Provide well-drained potting compost and plenty of light. Sun. **Hardiness** Hardy but needs good winter drainage to prevent the plant from rotting.

See page 74

Eucomis bicolor

An impressive flowering bulb that can be used in permanent plantings for its broad strappy foliage, big flower spikes and large seedheads. Plants emptied out of pots at the end of the season can be planted in the garden. **Cultivation** Easily grown in fertile potting compost. Sun. **Hardiness** Surprisingly hardy for such an exotic looking flower. With good drainage and deep planting it will survive to -10°C (14°F).

See page 48

Euonymus fortunei 'Emerald 'n' Gold'

A reliable, if a little predictable, evergreen shrub. It is a tough plant that given reasonable care will thrive for many years in a pot as the mainstay of a permanent planting. The leaves take on reddish tints during the winter particularly if the plant is undernourished. **Cultivation** Trim to shape as and when needed. Feed regularly, particularly in permanent plantings. **Hardiness** Fully hardy.

See page 38

Hakonechloa macra

Though not as popular as its variegated form, the plain green species has a softness and grace not found in other forms. The wispy seedheads add to its charm. **Cultivation** Grow in cool conditions and keep moist. Sun/shade. **Hardiness** Fully hardy.

See page 68

Hakonechloa macra 'Aureola'

A low-growing grass whose bright yellow variegated leaves can be used to enliven a planting. As they mature, the leaves arch over, forming a soft mound that is ideal as an underplanting to larger plants. **Cultivation** Keep the potting compost moist and feed well. Keep out of scorching sun to prevent the leaves from being bleached. **Hardiness** Hardy.

See page 50

Fatsia japonica

Marvellous shiny foliage and a robust shape combine to make this a very good centrepiece for a planting. The broad leaves are a perfect foil for feathery or spiky textures. **Cultivation** Grow in a shady site out of strong winds and feed and water regularly to keep the leaves in good condition. Shade. **Hardiness** Withstands several degrees of frost but may be damaged by persistent low temperatures.

See page 114

G

Geranium 'Ann Folkard'

A vigorous perennial with trailing stems that will either tumble out of a pot or scramble their way up through the planting. Younger leaves are yellow-green, turning green as they age. **Cultivation** Once established in the pot it makes rapid growth and some of the shoots will have to be snipped off or redirected if they are not to overwhelm the rest of the plants. **Hardiness** Fully hardy.

See page 104

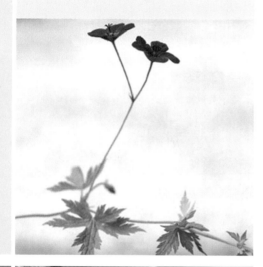

Hebe pimelioides 'Quicksilver'

A plant with tiny grey leaves and wiry black stems, this is unlikely to make you stand back in wonderment, but when used as an element of detail to build an overall richness to a planting it can be very effective. **Cultivation** The leaf colour is intensified by dry conditions. Full sun. **Hardiness** Hardy.

See page 74

Hedera helix 'Amber Waves'

This reliable and easy-to-grow evergreen develops dense trailing foliage that creeps over the rim of a pot, softening its edge. It provides good year-round colour. **Cultivation** Though tolerant of neglect, a good rich potting compost and regular feeding and watering produces a much healthier plant with better colour and therefore more impact. Sun or shade. **Hardiness** Fully hardy.

See page 90

Hedera helix 'Lalla Rookh'

A versatile plant that can be encouraged to climb, to trail or to grow flat across the top of the pot to provide an ornamental finish to the potting compost surface. **Cultivation** Water and feed regularly. Hederas are tolerant plants so prune, train and pinch out stems whenever there is a need. **Hardiness** Fully hardy.

See page 90

Helichrysum italicum

An evergreen shrub with narrow curry-scented leaves. Good for year-round effect. **Cultivation** Enjoys hot and dry conditions. Poor soil will result in a more intense silver colour. To keep its size in check, cut back any time between spring and late summer. **Hardiness** Likely to be damaged at temperatures below -6 or -7°C (23-21°F). It is likely to be more tolerant of cold if the potting compost is kept on the dry side.

See page 58

Helichrysum petiolare

This is an essential trailing container plant that can be used in many situations. It flows over the edge of a pot with style and its neat, felted leaves are a foil for a wide variety of colours and textures. **Cultivation** A vigorous tender perennial that enjoys regular feeding. Cut out unwanted or misplaced shoots when required. **Hardiness** To over-winter successfully it needs 7°C (45°F) minimum. It is best bought in new each spring.

See page 44, 110

Helichrysum petiolare 'Limelight'

This is one of my top five container plants. **Cultivation** It needs to be well fed and watered to look its best. Hot scorching sun will bleach and distort the leaves so keep it in light shade to get the best from the foliage. **Hardiness** Over-wintered plants often look scruffy and young plants grow away quickly so it is better to buy in new plants each year.

See page 44, 66

I

Impatiens 'Accent Cranberry'

Most Impatiens have harsh colours that are difficult to place in a display. 'Cranberry' is a far easier plant to use and ideal for richly coloured displays. **Cultivation** Tolerates sun if kept well watered but prefers a shady site or the shade from surrounding plants. Sun/shade. **Hardiness** Frost-tender perennial that can be over-wintered as a houseplant, otherwise buy in each year.

See page 88

Impatiens 'Accent White'

Except for the snowdrop, no plant has such a pure crystalline white flower. The perfect combination of its flower colour and rich green leaves puts this in my top five container plants. **Cultivation** Tolerates hot sun if kept well watered but prefers a shady site or the shade from surrounding plants. **Hardiness** Frost-tender perennial that can be over-wintered as a houseplant or bought new each year.

See page 36

Heuchera 'Can-can'

Dark purple foliage is useful for giving visual weight to the base of a planting. 'Can-can' is ideal for this task especially in hardy, all-year-round plantings. **Cultivation** Feed and water regularly and keep out of cold winter winds. It may be damaged by vine weevils. Sun or shade. **Hardiness** Hardy.

See page 34

Heuchera 'Plum Pudding'

'Plum Pudding' holds up well against winter weather and is one of the best Heucheras for winter effect. **Cultivation** Feed and water regularly and keep out of cold winter winds. May be damaged by vine weevils. Sun or shade. **Hardiness** Hardy.

See page 96

Heuchera 'Silver Scrolls'

Heucheras are amongst the best foliage plants for hardy container gardening. 'Silver Scrolls' is just one of many dark or marbled-leaved varieties. All are worth trying. Their persistent flower stalks can add useful vertical height to a planting. **Cultivation** Keep out of drying winds and do not let the potting compost dry out. May be damaged by vine weevils. Sun or shade. **Hardiness** Hardy.

See page 84

Imperata cylindrica 'Rubra'

A stunning perennial grass with green leaves that quickly mature to deep red. **Cultivation** This plant enjoys rich potting compost so incorporate plenty of organic matter and feed and water well. **Hardiness** I have had little success over-wintering this plant outdoors, so now I give it frost protection and keep it just moist and it comes through winter successfully.

See page 88

Ipomoea batatas 'Blackie'

Another of my top five plants. Use this small, compact plant on its own for its wonderful combination of foliage, shape, and colour, or mix it into small-scale displays. It does not climb. **Cultivation** Keep moist and well fed. Propagate from cuttings. Sun or shade. **Hardiness** Give a winter temperature of at least 7-8°C. (45-46°F).

See page 32, 94

Isoplexis canariensis

The way this plant presents its colour on upright flower spikes is useful to the container gardener. Trained as a standard it gives instant height to a display but it is equally good as low, leafy plant at the base of a planting. **Cultivation** An easily grown plant given an open sunny site and a well-fed potting compost. Sun. **Hardiness** A tender perennial needing a minimum winter temperature of 5°C (41°F).

See page 100

Isotoma (Laurentia) axillaris

A pretty plant with a gentle nature and useful as a fluffy filler amongst stronger plants or to create a romantic mood with pinks and whites. **Cultivation** An annual that succeeds in any reasonable potting compost that is not kept too wet. Sun. **Hardiness** This a tender annual that should not be put out until the risk of frost has passed.

See page 52

J

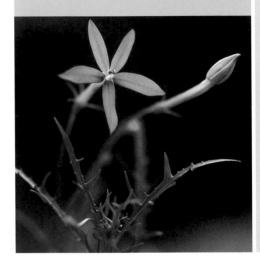

Juncus effusus f. spiralis

A tangle of a plant with glossy cylindrical stems twisted and curled in any number of ways. Good for year-round effect. **Cultivation** Its natural habitat is one of moist or even wet acid soil so regular watering and a neutral to acidic potting compost are important. Snip out old brown stems with scissors to prevent the plant from looking scruffy. **Hardiness** Hardy.

See page 34

L

Lamium galeobdolon 'Hermann's Pride'

A spreading perennial with silver netted foliage and hooded yellow flowers on erect stems. **Cultivation** Given moist potting compost, it makes a dense vigorous mat of foliage. The flowers can be left or cut off depending on your colour scheme. Shade. **Hardiness** Hardy.

See page 68

Lavandula 'Fathead'

Their tolerance of dry conditions makes Lavenders good container plants. This is a fairly compact plant with dumpy almost round flowerheads but there are dozens of different-sized and coloured varieties available. **Cultivation** Provide a sunny site and well-drained potting compost. Cut off flower stalks after flowering. To keep in shape, trim back into the previous season's growth but not into old wood, in spring. **Hardiness** Hardy given good drainage.

See page 28

K

Kalanchoe tomentosa

A textural delight. Useful for thoughtful plantings where tactile surfaces and shape are important. **Cultivation** Tolerates dry conditions but will grow more quickly with regular summer watering. **Hardiness** A tender succulent that requires minimum winter temperature of between 10-12°C (50-54°F) and plenty of light.

See page 72

Kleinia senecioides

Another of my top five plants. It has glaucous fleshy fingers on a vigorous trailing plant that can reach 70cm (28in) or more in a season. **Cultivation** Despite its drought-tolerant look water it regularly and it will respond by growing rapidly. **Hardiness** A frost-tender perennial needing a winter temperature of at least 5°C (50°F) and plenty of light.

See page 74, 112

Leymus arenarius

A dramatic perennial plant with coarse, powder blue, grassy leaves. Its invasive nature can be a nuisance but given a pot to itself its distinctive style can be used to advantage where a clean and sharp effect is needed. Cut off the unattractive seedheads. **Cultivation** Very tolerant of hot dry conditions and poor soil and does not enjoy over-wet potting compost. Sun. **Hardiness** Hardy.

See page 42, 110

Liriope muscari 'Variegata'

This evergreen perennial has a much brighter creamy yellow variegation than this picture shows and is a very showy plant. Good for year-round effect in shady conditions. An added bonus is the dense upright heads of small mauve flowers that are produced in late summer and autumn. **Cultivation** Dislikes wet potting compost and tolerates dryness surprisingly well for such a lush-looking plant. Shade. **Hardiness** Hardy.

See page 68

Lotus hirsutus

This is in my top-ten plants for its soft foliage and pink-tinged white flowers. They make it an effective foil for a wide range of colours and textures. **Cultivation** Best grown quite hard to keep it compact because too rich a potting compost causes straggly growth and less intense leaf colour as has tended to happen in my container plantings. Sun. **Hardiness** Hardy to -10°C (14°F) or lower in free draining, dry conditions.

See page 62

Lotus maculatus

A tender, perennial, trailing plant valuable for both its orange flowers and its feathery leaves. Young plants can put on 60cm (24in) or more growth by the end of the season. **Cultivation** An early summer flowering is usually followed by a reduced display before a late summer flourish. For the best display, do not let this plant dry out. Feed well. Sun. **Hardiness** Provide a minimum winter temperature of 5°C (41°F).

See page 86

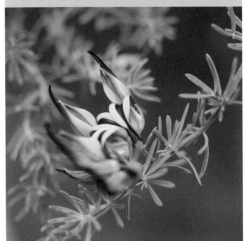

M

Melianthus major

This plant is right at the top of my list of all time greats for large containers. It has very dramatic large leaves getting greyer as they mature and with an interesting smell of peanut butter. **Cultivation** Responds well to feeding. Prone to whitefly in the greenhouse. Give it plenty of space. Sun. **Hardiness** Tolerates a few degrees of frost but best above 5°C (41°F) for the winter.

See page 110

O

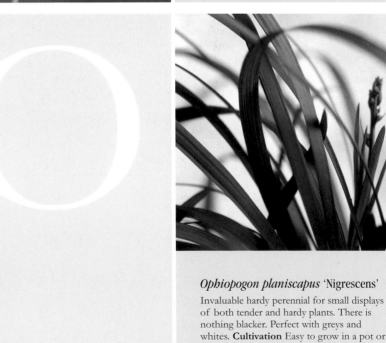

Ophiopogon planiscapus 'Nigrescens'

Invaluable hardy perennial for small displays of both tender and hardy plants. There is nothing blacker. Perfect with greys and whites. **Cultivation** Easy to grow in a pot or to bring on in the garden for container use. Splits readily into small tufts for tucking into your display. Sun or shade. **Hardiness** Hardy.

See page 32, 56, 84

Opuntia lindheimeri

Because of their adaptations to extreme environments, succulents are some of the most structural and elemental plants available. Not easy to use in combinations, they are often best displayed as individual specimens. **Cultivation** Use a free-draining soil-based potting compost and water regularly during the summer. Sun. **Hardiness** Withstands several degrees of frost providing it has very free drainage.

See page 76

Mimulus aurantiacus

An open and lax shrub with shiny sticky leaves. Few other plants can offer the same soft colouring. Darker and paler varieties are available and all are good plants. **Cultivation** Overwinter in a dry atmosphere to discourage rotting. Pinch out the growing tips to encourage a more bushy habit. Sun. **Hardiness** Provide a winter temperature between 8°-10°C (48-50°F).

See page 86

N

Nicotiana 'Lime Green'

There are many colours of annual bedding Nicotianas but few as distinctive as this. Bear in mind it grows to 50-60cm (20-24in) when planting young plants into a display. All are easy plants to grow. **Cultivation** Raise from seeds sown in spring or buy young plants. Deadhead regularly to encourage more flowers. Sun or light shade. **Hardiness** Plant out after the frosts are finished.

See page 48

Osteospermum jucundum

A vigorous spreading plant the produces flowers non-stop from late spring until the first frosts of winter. Its low mats of grey tinted, evergreen foliage make this a good plant for permanent planting. **Cultivation** Feed and water regularly. Make sure the pot drains freely if using in a year-round planting. Sun. **Hardiness** Possibly the toughest of all the Osteospermums. With good drainage it stands temperatures as low as -8 or -10°C (12-14°F).

See page 66, 96

Osteospermum 'Serena'

There is a wide range of Osteospermums now available including pinks and purples, yellows and white. All are good floriferous plants and the newer compact varieties are particularly good for small arrangements. I particularly like the subtlety of this variety's fragile, pink-brown colour. **Cultivation** Deadhead for continuous flowering. Sun or light shade. **Hardiness** Protect from frost.

See page 82, 86

P

Pelargonium 'Bushfire'

This is a regal pelargonium of moderately upright growth. Regal pelargoniums generally have fewer larger flowers and tougher toothed leaves than the more common zonal pelargoniums. **Cultivation** Deadhead regularly to prevent spent petals falling onto the leaves and causing rot. Sun. **Hardiness** Provide a minimum winter temperature of between 8 and 10°C (46-50°F).

See page 60

Pelargonium 'Harvard'

The trailing or ivy-leaved pelargoniums are substantial foliage plants as well as having good flowers. 'Harvard' has rich, regal red flowers and can make 60cm (24in) or more growth by the end of the season. **Cultivation** Feed and water regularly. Deadhead as each truss of flowers goes over. **Hardiness** Provide a minimum winter temperature of 4°C (39°F).

See page 30

Pelargonium tomentosum

Velvet-like leaves that smell of peppermint when rubbed, make this one of my favourite foliage plants. It is vigorous and can make 70cm (28in) or more spreading growth in a season. Flowers are small and not significant. Good in large containers or on its own spilling out of a low flat planter. **Cultivation** Easily grown. Sun or light shade. **Hardiness** Provide a minimum winter temperature of 4°C (39°F).

See page 100

Penstemon 'Blackbird'

There are many varieties of hybrid Penstemons, all are floriferous and all make good container plants. Colours range from purple to pink and white. 'Blackbird' is one of the darkest. Though usually reliable it flowered poorly in my container display. **Cultivation** Cut out spent flower stems to promote new flowering shoots. For protection do not remove top growth until after the winter. **Hardiness** Stands several degrees of frost especially if well drained.

See page 104

Persicaria microcephala

A leafy perennial with a spreading habit and growing to 30cm (12in) or so in height. A good filler around more floriferous plants. **Cultivation** Enjoys moist potting compost and a situation out of scorching midday sun. Sun/half-shade. **Hardiness** Hardy.

See page 82

Pelargonium Ignescens

It is worth looking beyond the usual regal and zonal pelargoniums and discovering the rest of the species and their close hybrids. There is a diverse range of leaf shapes and flower colours. *P.* 'Ignescens' is a primary hybrid with an upright open habit and flowers of intense fiery red. **Cultivation** Water, feed and deadhead regularly. Sun. **Hardiness** Provide a minimum winter temperature of 4°C (39°F).

See page 60

Pelargonium 'Lady Plymouth'

Another top ten plant. Unbeatable variegated foliage on a robust, easily satisfied, leafy and compact plant – what more could you ask for? Scent? Then you have it. Rub the leaves for a spicy eucalyptus smell. The pink flowers are small and should be ignored or removed. **Cultivation** Water, feed and deadhead regularly. Sun or shade. **Hardiness** Provide a minimum winter temperature of 4°C (39°F).

See page 98, 114

Pelargonium 'Sassy Dark Red'

I like this plant for its, compact habit, propensity to flower and its intensity of colour. Fully saturated colours like this cannot help but hold the attention. **Cultivation** Water, feed and deadhead regularly. Sun. **Hardiness** Provide a minimum winter temperature of 4°C (39°F).

See page 60

Persicaria microcephala 'Red Dragon'

A superb foliage plant despite its vigorous growth. In large pots it finds its way through other plants sending out shoots in unexpected places. Makes an attractive specimen in a pot on its own. **Cultivation** A herbaceous perennial that needs a moist potting compost and regular feeding. In poor conditions the leaves go brown and lose their lustre. Cut back wayward shoots at any time. Sun/shade. **Hardiness** Hardy.

See page 30

Petasites japonicus 'Nishiki-buki'

This is a very imposing garden thug. Well fed plants produce leaves up to 60cm (24in) across. Its spreading shoots are unstoppable in the garden. Containing it in a pot is the only way to enjoy it in a small garden. **Cultivation** Give it plenty of water and feed to realise its full glory. Tolerates sun but soon wilts in a small pot. Sun/Shade. **Hardiness** Hardy.

See page 102

Petunia 'Blue Trailing'

Good blue-flowered container plants are rare and should be cherished. This blue Petunia has a good balance of flower and foliage that prevents it from dominating the planting. **Cultivation** Regular dead-heading ensures continuity of flowering and also keeps the plant tidy. Sun. **Hardiness** Treat as an annual. Do not plant out if there is a danger of frost and discard at the end of the season.

See page 62

Petunia 'Million Bells' Red

Petunias and their close relatives come in all sizes. These small-flowered Petunias have considerably more charm than their larger counterparts and are easier to use in smaller, more intimate arrangements. **Cultivation** They do not enjoy over-wet potting compost so take care when watering. Sun. **Hardiness** Treat as an annual. Do not plant out if there is a danger of frost and discard at the end of the season.

See page 50

Petunia 'Million Bells' Cherry

A rich colour on a small attractive plant. Ideal for squeezing in amongst leafy plants to add highlights of colour. **Cultivation** Slightly prone to rotting at the beginning of the season if kept too wet and cold. Dead-heading is a beneficial though a rather fiddly job. Sun. **Hardiness** Treat as an annual. Do not plant out if there is a danger of frost and discard at the end of the season.

See page 50

Petunia 'Prism Sunshine'

A flower for soft effect. Plant breeders have developed large-flowered Petunias that are much more resistant to wind and rain than they used to be and this type has proved particularly reliable for me. **Cultivation** As with all Petunias regular dead-heading is beneficial. Sun/light shade. **Hardiness** Treat as an annual. Do not plant out if there is a danger of frost and discard at the end of the season.

See page 54, 70

Phormium hybrid

There is an ever-growing range of variegated hybrid Phormiums. Colours range from almost black to pink and bright yellow. The combination of colours and strong architectural qualities makes them very valuable to the container gardener. **Cultivation** Give them a free-draining potting compost but water well in the summer. Sun/light shade. **Hardiness** With good drainage and a sheltered position they are likely to tolerate temperatures to -5°C (23°F).

See page 40

Phormium tenax

This is one of the most imposing plants to use as the centrepiece of an arrangement. It is potentially a very large plant but in a container its growth rate is controlled and it can be kept small enough for many years. **Cultivation** Its tall evergreen leaves act like sails so beware of siting it in exposed positions. Sun/light shade. **Hardiness** Tolerates -5°C (23°F) and lower if kept dry and protected from cold winds.

See page 84

Phormium tenax 'Variegatum'

A striking evergreen plant with stiffly erect leaves. Ideal for structural year-round, permanent arrangements. **Cultivation** Give it a sunny position. Ensure a free-draining potting compost and water well in summer. Sun. **Hardiness** With good drainage and a sheltered position it is likely to tolerate temperatures at least to -5°C (23°F), possibly lower.

See page 68

Petunia 'Trailing Red'

I chose this Petunia for its intense colour. It is always better to buy your plants in flower so you know exactly what colour you are getting. Labels can be misleading. **Cultivation** Regular dead-heading ensures continuity of flowering and also keeps the plant tidy. Sun. **Hardiness** Treat as an annual. Do not plant out if there is a danger of frost and discard at the end of the season.

See page 38

Petunia 'Trailing White'

Trailing Petunias and their relatives Surfinia are prolific plants and valuable providers of bold blocks of colour. But take care not to let their mass of flowers overwhelm the rest of the planting. Be prepared to cut out whole stems to maintain balance in the display. **Cultivation** Deadhead regularly. Sun/light shade. **Hardiness** Treat as an annual. Do not plant out if there is a danger of frost and discard at the end of the season.

See page 44

Petunia 'White'

This is near the top of my list of flowers for cool and romantic effect. The purity of its whiteness stands out. **Cultivation** Keep it out of areas that are exposed to strong winds. Control slugs and snails that enjoy eating the flowers. Sun, light shade. **Hardiness** Treat as an annual. Do not plant out if there is a danger of frost and discard at the end of the growing season.

See page 54

Plectranthus argentatus

A textural delight. Its neutral colour works well with all sorts of other colours. Its soft lilac flowers are held in open heads. Evergreen. **Cultivation** Give it plenty of light but avoid windy sites. The stems are likely to snap as the plant gets bigger. Pinching out the shoot tips at regular intervals encourages bushy growth and a compact plant. Sun. **Hardiness** Needs a winter temperature between 8°-10°C (46-50°F).

See page 74

Plectranthus ciliatus

This plant has never flowered for me but that does not diminish its value as a good evergreen foliage plant. It has a trailing habit and can make 60cm (24in) or more in a season. Its effect is dark but that makes it the ideal foil for whites and silvers. **Cultivation** Keep it watered and well-fed and out of scorching sunshine. Sun/shade. **Hardiness** Give it a winter minimum temperature of around 8°C (46°F).

See page 74

Plectranthus madagascariensis 'Variegated Mintleaf'

Often labelled as Plectranthus Variegated, this is a far easier plant than the more traditional "trailing nepeta" (*Glechoma hederacea* 'Variegata') which always suffers from mildew in my plantings. The fleshy leaves are more substantial, the arching stems more elegant and the crisp variegation gives the whole plant more sparkle. **Cultivation** An easy and trouble-free plant. Sun/shade. **Hardiness** Over-winter at around 8°C (46°F).

See page 36, 98

Plectranthus zatarbendii

The is a low-growing, pot-hugging, identical twin of *Plectranthus argentatus* (*see p179*). The vigorous trailing stems make over 60cm (24in) of growth if well cared for. **Cultivation** An undemanding plant. The trailing stems will root when in contact with the soil and can be a useful and easy source of new plants. Sun. **Hardiness** Over-winter at around 8°C (46°F).

See page 78

R

Rhodochiton atrosanguineus

A tender perennial climber with distinctive hanging flowers. **Cultivation** Raise it from spring-sown seed where no facilities exist for overwintering. Seedlings grow rapidly and soon make sizeable plants by early summer. Do not put plants outdoors until the danger of frost has gone. Provide twiggy support. Prone to attack by whitefly in the glasshouse. Sun. **Hardiness** Not hardy. Provide a winter minimum of 8°C (46°F).

See page 30, 78

Salvia splendens 'Purple'

A useful alternative to the usual bright red, dirty white or washy pink varieties. The stumpy growth is not elegant but it provides solid colour. **Cultivation** Raise from spring-sown seed or buy in. Sun. **Hardiness** Treat as a half-hardy annual. Discard at the end of the season.

See page 46

Sambucus nigra 'Black Lace'

A hardy deciduous shrub that is unremarkable in the winter, but in summer its deeply-cut purple foliage is extremely useful for a wispy effect. **Cultivation** At the end of the season, remove the plant from its display and pot it into as small a pot as is practical. Prune it back to approximately 30cm (12in). Over-winter it outdoors then plant it into a new display in spring. Sun/shade. **Hardiness** Fully hardy.

See page 30, 38

Senecio macroglossus 'Variegatus'

Here is another houseplant ideal for outdoor ornamental use. Given the benefit of a large container and the warmth of summer, its growth outdoors is rapid. **Cultivation** Do not plant out until the risk of frost has passed. Provide support for the twining stems. Sun/shade. **Hardiness** Minimum winter temperature of 7°C (45°F).

See page 54

S

Salvia 'Raspberry Royale'

An open, twiggy, semi-evergreen shrub. The branches are brittle so handle with care. **Cultivation** To reuse this shrub, dig it out of its display at the end of the season and pot it up. It tolerates a few degrees of frost but it is safer to keep it frost-free during the winter. In spring, cut back the branches to about 20cm (8in) before planting into a new display. Sun. **Hardiness** Withstands some frost.

See page 112

Salvia farinacea 'Victoria'

Valuable for its bushy foliage, the rich colour of its flowers and its upright line. **Cultivation** Although this is a tender herbaceous perennial it is better treated as an annual. Raise new plants from seed sown in late winter or spring. Young plants are freely available at garden centres in early summer. Sun. **Hardiness** Do not plant out until the danger of frost has gone. It continues to flower until the first hard frost.

See page 104

Senecio petasitis

A large, velvet-leaved plant that produces big heads of small yellow flowers on mature plants. It needs to be touched for the full sensory experience. **Cultivation** Removing the growing tips when young encourages branching and suckering from the roots. **Hardiness** Withstands the first few frosts but ideally should be kept frost-free during the winter.

See page 98

Silene uniflora 'Swan Lake'

A tough plant whose small blue leaves and long flower stems give elegance to the double pompom flowers. **Cultivation** Requires sunshine and good drainage. This plant grows in seaside conditions so tolerates wind, sun and dryness but becomes a far better plant if treated more generously. It dislikes winter water-logging. Sun. **Hardiness** Hardy.

See page 42

Solanum rantonnetii

An ornamental evergreen shrubby member of the potato family. **Cultivation** Trained as a standard in the container portrait (*see page 52*), it works equally well as a small shrub, although it needs a large pot. Regularly pinching out the growing tips keeps it compact and ensures plenty of new shoots and an abundance of flowers. Feed and water regularly. Sun. **Hardiness** Over-winter at a temperature of at least 7°C (45°F).

See page 52

Solenostemon 'Midnight'

Leaves of Solenostemon (Coleus) varieties range from whole to so deeply lobed and twisted as to appear shredded. 'Midnight' is as scallop-edged as I like to go. **Cultivation** If kept moist it will tolerate full sun. Large plants tend to snap in very windy conditions. Cuttings root easily – putting them in a glass of water on a window-sill works perfectly well. Sun/shade. **Hardiness** Provide a winter minimum of 7°C (45°F).

See page 38

Solenostemon 'Black Prince'

Single-coloured varieties are the easiest to work with. The matt finish to the leaves makes this variety especially effective in container displays. **Cultivation** The flowers of the Solenostemon are rather small and ineffective. They are best pinched out as they form. Sun/shade. **Hardiness** Provide a winter minimum of 7°C (45°F).

See page 62

Solenostemon hybrid

There are hundreds of named varieties of what are more commonly known as Coleus. Yet more unnamed hybrid seedlings are offered as mixed selections in garden centres. **Cultivation** Keep well-watered and feed regularly. Keep out of exposed sites because blustery winds can snap off the branches of larger plants. Pinch out flower buds. Sun/shade. **Hardiness** Provide a winter minimum temperature of 7°C (45°F).

See page 82

T

Tellima grandiflora 'Forest Frost'

An evergreen perennial with open spikes of green and pink flowers in late spring. The foliage takes on reddish tints in winter. **Cultivation** Cut out the flower stems as soon as they are over or before if they spoil the look of your display. Though tolerant of dry conditions, a better plant will result from regular watering and occasional feeding through the summer. Shade. **Hardiness** Hardy.

See page 64

Teucrium scorodonia 'Crispum'

An interesting evergreen sub-shrub with crinkly textured leaves. Ideal for hardy textural mixes. Its green flowers only add to its overall effect. **Cultivation** This is an easily satisfied plant, tolerant of shade and dry conditions, however, a much fresher-looking plant will be produced by regular watering and feeding. **Hardiness** Hardy.

See page 34

Solenostemon 'Juliet Quartermain'

Solenostemons provide some of the richest foliage colour but they need good light to be at their best. Look out for named varieties such as this that have been selected for their reliability and colour. **Cultivation** Keep well-watered and feed regularly. Keep out of exposed sites because wind can snap off the branches of larger plants. Pinch out growing tips to encourage bushiness. Take off flower buds. Sun/shade. **Hardiness** Provide a winter minimum temperature of 7°C (45°F).

See page 106

Solenostemon 'Winter Sun'

Well-grown specimens of Solenostemon, particularly the single-coloured varieties, have sufficient character to stand alone as specimens. They are quick-growing given plenty of light and rich potting compost. **Cultivation** To produce high quality plants, feed weekly with a balanced plant food and make sure that the plant does not dry out . Keep out of buffeting winds and pinch out young flower buds. Sun/shade. **Hardiness** Provide a winter minimum of 7°C (45°F).

See page 40

Sphaeralcea 'Newleaze Coral'

A sun-loving open and upright sub–shrub. The mallow-like flowers are produced from early summer until the first frosts. **Cultivation** Needs well-drained potting compost and a sunny position. **Hardiness** With good drainage and a sheltered position it withstands several degrees of frost but if possible, give it frost protection to be safe.

See page 60

Thunbergia alata

This cheerful climbing plant is very useful for background height in a container. Given a long growing season it makes over 1.5m (5ft). In shorter arrangements, wrap the stems back on each other **Cultivation** This is a tender perennial plant that is usually treated as an annual. Raise from seed sown indoors in spring. It dislikes cold so plant out after the frosts have gone and the temperature has warmed up. Sun. **Hardiness** Over-winter at 7°C (45°F) minimum.

See page 54, 108

Tibouchina urvilleana

One of the top plants for a flamboyant effect, on account of its large exotic-coloured flowers. The foliage is covered in soft down. **Cultivation** It can make a large shrub with a framework of stout branches and is ideal as a single specimen but is also tolerant of being cut back each spring to bring it down to manageable proportions for a mixed display. Sun. **Hardiness** Give a winter minimum of 5°C (43°F).

See page 104

Tolmiea menziesii 'Taff's Gold'

A leafy perennial valuable for its shade-tolerant foliage that makes a luxuriant clump when well fed and watered. The early-season flower spikes have little impact as a design feature but reveal a complex mix of brown, pink, purple, orange and green filamentous flowers when studied close up. **Cultivation** An easily satisfied plant given moisture, shade and a rich potting compost. Shade. **Hardiness** Hardy.

See page 102

Tradescantia pallida 'Purpurea'

A popular houseplant but rarely used outdoors which is a pity because it is an extremely useful foliage plant for container gardening. **Cultivation** The foliage has a bloom that is easily rubbed off so take care when handling. Splashes of hard water also dry to leave disfiguring marks. Sun/shade. **Hardiness** Tolerates the first frosts but then it needs bringing in to a winter temperature of around 10°C (50°F).

See page 94

U

Uncinia rubra

A richly coloured evergreen grass that is lovely when young but becomes straggly after a few seasons so use young plants for best effect. **Cultivation** Grow in a fertile free draining compost but keep moist in the summer. Sun. **Hardiness** Tolerates several degrees of frost when grown in well-drained conditions.

See page 80

Verbena Tapien Violet

There are many seed strains of Verbena. Some are trailing plants others are erect and bushy. I chose this Verbena for its rich colour and trailing habit. To be sure you get the colour you require buy your plants in flower. **Cultivation** Dead-heading is important for successive flowering. Sun. Prone to attack by aphids. **Hardiness** Grow as an annual. Plant out after the last frost and discard at the end of the season.

See page 44, 46

Vinca minor 'Illumination'

A variegated variety of the common Periwinkle. Its evergreen quality makes it ideal for year-round displays. Slower growing than its all-green counterpart, its stems still trail up to 40-50cm (16-20in) long in a season. With me, it does not produce many flowers. They are blue and can either be left on or pinched off if they upset your colour scheme. **Cultivation** A tough plant and easy to care for. Sun. **Hardiness** Hardy.

See page 50

Viola 'Apricot'

Violas are good for providing bold patches of colour, particularly during the winter when nothing else is flowering. The summer varieties like 'Apricot' give a relaxed, cottage feel to a planting. Avoid mixed colours if you want a unified and designed look. **Cultivation** Look out for damage by aphids. Sun. **Hardiness** A tough plant that will often last more than a season but is best discarded at the end of the summer.

See page 86

V

Verbena 'Aztec Red Trailing'

It was the intensity of its colour that attracted me to this vigorous trailing variety. Few other plants offer such a pure red. **Cultivation** Dead-heading is important for successive flowering. Keep well fed and watered. Plants under drought stress are susceptible to mildew. Aphids can be a problem so check regularly. Sun. **Hardiness** Grow as an annual. Plant out after the last frost and discard at the end of the season.

See page 38

Verbena 'Diamond Merci'

This is a vigorous trailing variety with good disease resistance and a rich burgundy colour that is unusual amongst Verbenas. **Cultivation** Dead-heading is important for successive flowering. Prone to attack by aphids. Benefits from regular feeding. Sun. **Hardiness** Grow as an annual. Plant out after the last frost and discard at the end of the season.

See page 46

Viola 'Bowles' Black'

A useful plant for adding touches of distinction to small displays. **Cultivation** It is a short-lived plant and best treated as an annual or biennial. For continuous flowering it is important not to let it set seed and to dead-head regularly. Prone to attacks by aphids which distort and stunt the growth. Mildew is sometimes a problem. Sun. **Hardiness** Hardy.

See page 46, 62

useful suppliers

PLANT SUPPLIERS

Dibley's Nurseries
LLanelidan
Ruthin,
Denbighshire
LL15 2LG
Tel: 01978 790677
www.dibleys.com
email sales@dibleys.com

Fibrex Nurseries Limited
Honeybourne Road
Pebworth
Stratford-upon-Avon
Warwickshire
CVB37 8XP
Tel: 01789 720788
www.fibrex.co.uk
email sales@fibrex.co.uk

Kobakoba
2 High Street
Ashcroft
Bridgwater
Somerset
TA7 9PL
Tel: 01458 210700
www.kobakoba.co.uk
email plants@kobakoba.co.uk

Mill Lane Nurseries
Mill Lane,
Cleeve Prior
Evesham,
Worcs.
WR11 8JZ

Tel: 01789 773231
www.mill-lane-nurseries.co.uk
email: info@mill-lane-nurseries.co.uk

Trevena Cross Nurseries
Breage
Helston
Cornwall
TR13 9PS
Tel: 01736 763 880
www.trevenacross.co.uk

HARD-LANDSCAPING MATERIALS

Formica Limited
Coast Road
North Shields
Tyne & Wear
NE29 8RE
Tel: 0191 259 3000
www.formica-europe.com

Stoneage Limited
Unit 3
Parson's Green Depot
Parson's Green Lane
London
SW6 7HH
Tel: 020 7384 9090
www.estone.co.uk

Stonemarket Limited
Oxford Road
Ryton-on-Dunsmore
Warwickshire
CV8 3E
Tel: 024 7651 8700
www.stonemarket.co.uk

Thatch International Limited
The Natural Range
Stonefield Park
Chilbolton
Stockbridge
Hampshire
SO20 6BL

Tel: 0845 600 9292
www.thatch.co.uk

CONTAINER SUPPLIERS

Gaze Burvill Limited
Redloh House
2 Michael Road
London
SW6 2AD
Tel: 020 7471 8500
www.gazeburvill.com

see pages 25 (top), 92-93

Designers and builders of high quality outdoor furniture and solid wood planters in steam-bent oak.

Inside Out
Wallcrouch
Wadhurst
East Sussex
TN5 7JL
Tel: 01580 200 399
www.insideout-ornaments.co.uk

see pages 24, 44-45

Suppliers of Cretan terracotta pots and urns, antique and traditional, plus beautiful fake lead planters. Retail and trade welcome.

Iota Garden and Home Limited
24 South Road
Portishead
Bristol
BS20 7DW
Tel 01275 840 195
www.iotagarden.co

see pages 32-33, 106-107 (pots in foreground)

A fantastic range of contemporary stone containers, plus reflecting features in mirrored stainless steel.

Mark Pedro de la Torre
The Courtyard
Old Rectory
Stoke Lacy
Herefordshire
HR7 4HH
Tel: 01432 820500
www.markpedrodelatorre.com

see pages 12, 17 (middle image), 22
(middle image)

Beautifully crafted terracotta and metal pots in contemporary and original shapes and finishes.

Obbligato
POBox 190
Pinetown 3600
South Africa
Tel: +27 31 700 6565
www.obbligato.co.za

see pages 40-41, 76-77 (aluminium pot
in background)

Contemporary steel, copper, aluminium, and perspex plant pots in various sizes and shapes. Ideal for succulents, cacti and other low-maintenance plants.

Outdoor Design
John Booth Engineering Ltd
Unit 1, Block A
Ford Airfield Industrial Estate
Ford
Arundel
West Sussex
BN18 OHY
Tel: 01903 716960
www.outdoordesign.co.uk

see pages 60-61, 76-77 (galvanised metal
group in foreground), 80-81, 104-105,
112-113

Offers a broad range of steel garden planters, both traditional and contemporary, in a choice of different finishes.

Prestige Plants
Columbine Hall Nursery
Stowupland
Suffolk
IP14 4AT
Tel: 01449 615919
www.prestigeplants.co.uk

see pages 100-101, 108-109, 140-141

Superb range of resin planters imitating the finest Italian terracotta.

Pret-a-pot
6a Cow Lane
Sidlesham
West Sussex
PO20 7LN
Tel: 01243 641928
www.pret-a-pot.co.uk

see pages 20, 28-29, 30-31, 48-49, 68-69,
78-79, 88-89, 94-95 (metal trough on
wall), 106-107 (pot in background)

Offers a contemporary collection of planters in metal and ceramic ranging from 10mm to 1000mm. Suitable for interior and exterior use.

Urbis Design
City Studios
Alpha House
London E8 2ND
Tel: 0207 254 0601
www.urbisdesign.co.uk

see pages 25 (middle image), 56-57, 74-75

Curvy contemporary design. Garden planters and furniture with stylish, pure forms and an inspired range of colours and finishes.

Whichford Pottery
Whichford
Shipston-on-Stour
Warwickshire
CV36 5PG
Tel: 01608 684416
www.whichfordpottery.com

see pages 23, 34-35, 62-63, 72-73, 84-85,
86-87, 98-99, 118

Hand-thrown and moulded terracotta pots in a host of traditional and contemporary designs to suit all tastes.

Loaned by the author

see pages 46-47, 54-55, 90-91, 94-95
(recycled copper pot in foreground)

index

Acknowledgements

The author would like to give special thanks to Robin, Bella and John for their relentless efforts through a blisteringly hot summer. Special thanks also to Craig Knowles and his very able assistants. We had a good summer. A big thanks to the whole team at Whichford Pottery and to the ever helpful and enthusiastic ladies at Fibrex Nurseries. Many thanks all.

The publisher's would like to thank Roger Hughes at Stonemarket Ltd for all the paving and edging materials that enabled us to build our elaborate outdoor stages. To Samantha Dawe at The Think Tank for co-ordinating delivery of Formica finishes. To Robert Norris at Thatch International Ltd for the willow screening and wattle hurdles. We would also like to thank everyone who supplied us with containers including Adam Caplin for the loan of his teak planter and everyone at Evergreen, Covent Garden Flower Market.